CENTRE FOR EDUCATIONAL RESEARCH AND INNOVATION

Students with Disabilities, Learning Difficulties and Disadvantages

STATISTICS AND INDICATORS

OECD

ORGANISATION FOR ECONOMIC CO-OPERATION AND DEVELOPMENT

ORGANISATION FOR ECONOMIC CO-OPERATION AND DEVELOPMENT

The OECD is a unique forum where the governments of 30 democracies work together to address the economic, social and environmental challenges of globalisation. The OECD is also at the forefront of efforts to understand and to help governments respond to new developments and concerns, such as corporate governance, the information economy and the challenges of an ageing population. The Organisation provides a setting where governments can compare policy experiences, seek answers to common problems, identify good practice and work to co-ordinate domestic and international policies.

The OECD member countries are: Australia, Austria, Belgium, Canada, the Czech Republic, Denmark, Finland, France, Germany, Greece, Hungary, Iceland, Ireland, Italy, Japan, Korea, Luxembourg, Mexico, the Netherlands, New Zealand, Norway, Poland, Portugal, the Slovak Republic, Spain, Sweden, Switzerland, Turkey, the United Kingdom and the United States. The Commission of the European Communities takes part in the work of the OECD.

OECD Publishing disseminates widely the results of the Organisation's statistics gathering and research on economic, social and environmental issues, as well as the conventions, guidelines and standards agreed by its members.

This work is published on the responsibility of the Secretary-General of the OECD. The opinions expressed and arguments employed herein do not necessarily reflect the official views of the Organisation or of the governments of its member countries.

Publié en français sous le titre :
Élèves présentant des déficiences, des difficultés et des désavantages sociaux
Statistiques et indicateurs

Foreword

In the mid-nineties, the OECD's Centre for Educational Research and Innovation (CERI)[1] published a collection of data making comparisons in the field of special needs education in a number of OECD countries. This work strengthened the view that a different comparative framework would need to be developed if reliable and valid comparisons were to be made. Subsequent discussions with participating member countries identified a resource-based definition as the best means of facilitating international comparison. This helps to overcome currently different national interpretations of concepts such as special educational needs which cover very different populations of students who are experiencing difficulties in accessing the curriculum. It is not unproblematic, however, so in the longer run further work will be needed to try to develop and use common definitions of concepts, as has been done to advance the development and use of statistics and indicators in other areas of work on education.

Concurrent work at UNESCO and OECD in revising standards for classifying education systems (ISCED) updated the definition of special needs education and reformulated it to reflect policy developments. In doing so, a much wider range of students, in all types of schools were brought into the frame. In addition, the idea that extra resources may be needed to assist schools to help students access the curriculum more effectively was included in the new description.

In order for policy relevant comparisons to emerge, a resource-based approach would require that the students included under this definition would need to be sub-divided into some form of straightforward classification scheme. Participating countries agreed on a tri-partite system in which students are divided into three cross-national categories, A, B and C. Broadly, they cover:

- Students with disabilities or impairments viewed in medical terms as organic disorders attributable to organic pathologies (*e.g.* in relation to sensory, motor or neurological defects). The educational need is considered to arise primarily from problems attributable to these disabilities (cross-national category "A/Disabilities").

- Students with behavioural or emotional disorders, or specific difficulties in learning. The educational need is considered to arise primarily from problems in the interaction between the student and the educational context (cross-national category "B/Difficulties").

- Students with disadvantages arising primarily from socio-economic, cultural, and/or linguistic factors. The educational need is to compensate for the disadvantages attributable to these factors (cross-national category "C/Disadvantages").

---

1. CERI was created in June 1968 by the OECD Council, and all member countries of the OECD are participants. It is supervised by a Governing Board composed of one national expert in its field of competence from each of the countries participating in its programme of work.

It is in Category C that the resource-based definition is most problematic because the numbers of students in this category reflect both demand, based on student need, and supply, based on national capacity as well as willingness to provide support. The extent of supply can, therefore, depend on national wealth as well as national policy. It can also be influenced by the adequacy of the base-level resources in schools to deal with student disadvantage. The extent of demand can also vary between countries because of differences in the nature and levels of immigration and the impact of policies to overcome poverty.

Work to refine the concepts and definitions continues. Meanwhile, the data provided in this book are based on the application of the three categories as outlined above. This edition presents an updated (2000-2001) account of the development of the work, and provides qualitative data to contextualise the quantitative information. It provides breakdowns by national category systems as well as comparisons using the cross-national framework described.

The work was supported by contributions from the US Department of Education, Office of Special Education and Rehabilitative Services (OSERS) as well as by additional funds from the following participating countries: Belgium (Flemish Community), Canada (British Columbia and Saskatchewan), Finland, France, Germany, Greece (Hellenic American Union), Hungary, Ireland, Japan, Korea, Mexico, the Netherlands, Norway, the Slovak Republic, Spain, Sweden, Switzerland and Turkey.

The book was prepared by the chief consultant to the project, Colin Robson, Emeritus Professor, University of Huddersfield, and by Peter Evans and Marcella Deluca of the OECD/CERI secretariat, with the assistance of Philippe Hervé and James Bouch. The countries involved collaborated closely. This book is published under the responsibility of the Secretary-General of the OECD.

Barry McGaw

Director, Directorate for Education

Table of Contents

List of charts

List of tables

Chapter 1
Introduction

Background

The performance of national education systems is a topic which continues to receive a large amount of interest. All OECD member countries are concerned with the standards attained by students and the type of learning that all children and young people are engaged in, as educational reforms are planned and put in place as part of a strategy for moving countries into the knowledge economy.

Students with disabilities, learning difficulties and disadvantages are no exception, and programmes are being developed to assist these students to improve their skills and to be included more fully into society and work. The demographic trends are such that in the coming years, as a result of the increasing numbers of retired citizens and the decreasing birth rate, all available skills will be needed to maintain our economies.

The gathering of statistics and the development of indicators of education systems are viewed as indispensable to this endeavour, and the effort has been spearheaded by OECD in collaboration with UNESCO and the European Union. However, it has been noticeable that data on students who have difficulties in accessing the curriculum are more difficult to come by than for the rest of the student population.

In 1995, OECD published a first set of data intended to provide a comparative review of provision for students with disabilities and disadvantages in OECD countries. Although the work showed that the definitions used were so different among countries that comparisons were almost impossible to make, sufficiently large differences existed between countries to indicate the occurrence of substantial variations in provision.

This monograph follows on from this work and describes the continuation of a process which is intended to improve the quality of the database and international comparability. In this way policy making in the field of education for disabled and disadvantaged students will be better informed.

More recently, and providing additional motivation for a new initiative in this area, the instrument used for defining the nature of education statistics to be gathered internationally, the International Standard Classification of Education (ISCED), has been revised. In the original version of the classification, special education was defined as the education provided in special schools; a definition wholly out of keeping with both theory and practice in many countries, and which in itself limits interest in obtaining data in this area.

The most recent version of ISCED (ISCED 97) has attempted to put this right and provides the following definition of special education:

Special needs education – Educational intervention and support designed to address special educational needs. *The term "special needs education" has come into use as a replacement for the term "special education". The older term was mainly understood to refer to the education of children with disabilities that takes place in special schools or institutions distinct from, and outside of, the institutions of the regular school and university system. In many countries today a large proportion of disabled children are in fact educated in institutions of the regular system. Moreover, the concept of "children with special educational needs" extends beyond those who may be included in handicapped categories to cover those who are failing in school for a wide variety of other reasons that are known to be likely to impede a child's optimal progress. Whether or not this more broadly defined group of children are in need of additional support depends on the extent to which schools are able to adapt their curriculum, teaching and organisation and/or to provide additional human or material resources so as to stimulate efficient and effective learning for these pupils.* (UNESCO, 1997)

It is clear that this definition substantially changes and updates the definition of special education – particularly in terms of resources made available, and it carries with it a requirement for a rather different operationalisation for the purposes of gathering statistics.

As noted above, earlier work had identified the difficulty in comparing data in special needs education among countries. Two outstanding problems were identified. First, the term "special needs education" means different things in different countries. In some it covers only children with traditional disabilities, while in others it includes a broader range of students covering, for instance, disability, learning difficulty and disadvantage. Second, because of the wide variations in the definitions of disability and learning difficulty which are in use, the extent to which quantitative estimates for any particular category from different countries are comparable remains unclear. Furthermore, there has been in special educational circles particular concern about the lack of educational utility of descriptive categories which are derived from medical classifications. Disability categories are viewed as having only partial implications for educational provision or for the development of teaching programmes, which inevitably have to take the whole child into account. In this way, therefore, categories based on medical descriptions are at best of only limited value to education policy makers, who are the main audience for data gathered within the ISCED framework at OECD.

From special educational needs to disabilities, difficulties, disadvantages

It is clear that in an international setting the use of the term "special educational needs" leads to confusion because it means different things for different countries. As a result, except where necessary for historical reasons, the term is not used in this monograph. Instead the words disabilities, difficulties and disadvantages are used. These terms broadly describe the students for whom countries make additional resources available so that they can access the curriculum more effectively.

In addition, the data gathered on these students is presented separately for the three cross-national categories A, B and C (students with disabilities, difficulties and disadvantages respectively). It has been chosen to present the data in this way to facilitate educational policy–making. Although certainly there are some features in common across the three categories there are a number of issues that do not apply equally across all three categories; for instance, the place of education of students with disabilities (special schools, special classes, regular classes).

OECD countries provide additional resources to help students with disabilities, difficulties and disadvantages access the curriculum and benefit as fully as possible from education. Further analysis of how these resources are used and for whom and to what ends becomes key to understand whether education systems are as equitable as they should be. It is towards illuminating this goal that the data collection on these students is directed. Given the very different approaches taken by member countries of the OECD it is an area which should benefit from international comparisons.

The resource-based definition

The points raised above argue, then, for a new approach and following proposals from the Secretariat at OECD and in discussion with member countries it was decided to tackle the problem in the following way. In order to overcome the different definitions of special needs education that operate among countries, it was necessary to provide a means to identify and include all students for whom extra provision is made in order to help them make progress through the school curriculum.

It was decided to identify this envelope of students through a supply side approach based on resources made available. This has the advantage of being educationally based and at the same time fits with the intent of the ISCED 97 definition.

Thus, the definition of special needs education agreed is that "those with special educational needs are defined by the additional public and/or private resources provided to support their education". The use of this definition in a consistent manner calls for agreement about the term ADDITIONAL and an appreciation of the various kinds of possible RESOURCES PROVIDED which should be considered.

Thus "additional resources" are those made available over and above the resources generally available to students[1] where no consideration is given to needs of students likely to have particular difficulties in accessing the regular curriculum.

Resources can be of many different kinds. Examples are:

- PERSONNEL RESOURCES. These include a more favourable teacher/student ratio than in a regular classroom where no allowance is being made for students with special needs; additional teachers, assistants or any other personnel (for some or all of the time); training programmes for teachers and others which equip them for work in special needs education.

- MATERIAL RESOURCES. These include aids or supports of various types (*e.g.* hearing aid); modifications or adaptations to classroom; specialised teaching materials.

- FINANCIAL RESOURCES. These include funding formulae which are more favourable to those with special needs (including classes where it is known or assumed that there are students with special needs); systems where money is set aside for special educational needs within the regular budget allocation; payments made in support of special needs education; and the costs of personnel and material resources.

---

1. The term "student" is used. It is to be regarded as synonymous with "pupil" or "(school) child". When discussing pre-primary aged children the term child/children is used as "student" seems inappropriate for this age level.

The key question is whether these resources are made available to support their education and are provided when students have particular difficulties in accessing the regular curriculum.

One result of the resources approach is that it brings together students with learning difficulties with very different causes, and it was recognised that a group formed in this way would itself need to be further sub-divided. To achieve this, a tri-partite categorisation system was devised based on perceived causes of difficulty in accessing the regular curriculum. Countries are asked to re-classify the data into this framework based on the classification and data collection arrangements used in their own national system following the operational definitions provided.

Operational definitions of cross-national categories[2]

The three agreed cross-national categories are referred to as "A/Disabilities", "B/Difficulties" and "C/Disadvantages" respectively.

Cross-national category "A/Disabilities": students with disabilities or impairments viewed in medical terms as organic disorders attributable to organic pathologies (*e.g.* in relation to sensory, motor or neurological defects). The educational need is considered to arise primarily from problems attributable to these disabilities.

Cross-national category "B/Difficulties": students with behavioural or emotional disorders, or specific difficulties in learning. The educational need is considered to arise primarily from problems in the interaction between the student and the educational context.

Cross-national category "C/Disadvantages": students with disadvantages arising primarily from socio-economic, cultural, and/or linguistic factors. The educational need is to compensate for the disadvantages attributable to these factors.

The definition of special educational needs (SEN) given in the ISCED 97 manual and the derived resources definition have in practice presented problems for some countries. Specifically for example the association of students from ethnic minorities with those with special education needs clashes with some national policy frameworks and national understanding of the concept of SEN.

Given the roots of this work it is not straightforward to easily deal with this issue. Nevertheless the statistical analysis recognises the problem and in general analyses data for A, B and C separately unless it is clear that combining the data is useful, and the issue is taken up more fully in the final chapter where policy implications are drawn out.

In the following chapters, these ideas and descriptions are elaborated upon and data gathered within this new framework are presented.

- *Chapter 2* provides an analysis of the qualitative data.

- *Chapter 3* provides a comparative analysis of quantitative data based on categories used nationally to identify students who are in need of additional resources to help them access the curriculum.

---

2. These definitions are to be seen in the context of the resources definition. Allocation of national categories to a particular cross-national category is based on the reason for providing additional resources.

- *Chapter 4* provides an analysis of quantitative data for cross-national categories A, B, C.

- *Chapter 5* provides an additional analysis of the quantitative data, including gender and age distributions.

- *Chapter 6* provides discussion and conclusions.

The electronic questionnaire

An electronic questionnaire is used to gather data on students with disabilities, learning difficulties and disadvantages thus allowing the development of a database, and of a methodology and technology compatible with the general education statistics work undertaken by OECD. It was put together to take account of the wide variety of national systems in use which was highlighted in the initial phase and comprises:

- **Table 0** which requests information on any categories of students which are considered to fall within the resources definition and their classification into cross-national categories A, B or C.

- **Table 1** which asks for information on the starting and ending ages of various stages of education.

- **Table 2** which asks for information on number of students with special educational needs in special schools, on the institutions (public and private), numbers of classes and on the teaching staff.

- **Table 3** which asks for information on number of students with special needs in special classes, on the institutions (public and private), numbers of classes and on the teaching staff.

- **Table 4** which asks for information on number of students with special needs in regular classes, on the institutions (public and private), and numbers of classes.

- **Table 6**[3] which asks for information on all students enrolled in special educational programmes classified by age as well as on those not registered in the education system.

In addition, information on total numbers of students in each level of education including compulsory is requested as well as gender and age breakdowns.

The electronic questionnaire aims to simplify data collection and already available information is pre-entered individually for each country and thereby only needs checking during completion. Also, the requested coverage includes both pre-school and upper secondary education, since both of these phases of education are of considerable interest in relation to special educational needs provision and are necessary for providing a full picture of the education of these students. Other technical changes have been made to allow ultimately for data sets fully compatible with the new ISCED requirements. In particular, consideration for classification by programme content is allowed for.

The electronic questionnaire is designed so that the data requested are almost exclusively based on those already collected for other purposes, although not necessarily

---

3. There is no Table 5.

currently collated nationally. However, it may be feasible for central agencies in countries to provide different or additional breakdowns of statistics to those they currently produce; or to augment these data with statistics normally held only at regional or even local level.

The nature and sources of the database for this report

Twenty-two returns of the electronic questionnaire for school year 2000/2001 (but see following paragraphs for exceptions) were received from the following 21 countries and provinces: Belgium (Flemish Community and French Community), Canada (New Brunswick, district 18), the Czech Republic, Finland, France, Germany, Greece, Hungary, Italy, Japan, Korea, Mexico, the Netherlands, Poland, the Slovak Republic, Spain, Sweden, Switzerland, Turkey, the United Kingdom (England) and the United States.

Exceptions are Hungary and Mexico, for which data refer to the school year 1999/2000; and Canada (NB) and Greece, for which data refer to the school year 2001/2002. Sweden provided only qualitative data.

The data are provided by national authorities from databases already gathered in countries for administrative purposes. The work reported has benefited from close collaboration between the OECD/CERI Secretariat and country representatives and the data presented are therefore as accurate as possible.

Because it has not yet proved possible to use the programmatic definitions of the ISCED levels the terms pre-primary, primary, lower secondary and upper secondary are used as proxies for ISCED levels 0 to 3.

Data limitations

Despite increasing agreement about the cross-national definitions and growing adherence to these definitions among countries when allocating their individual country categories, there remain some divergences. Work is continuing on harmonising international reporting of these data. For example, the allocation of national categories to cross-national categories A, B and C is permanently under review. Work is also continuing to provide full data sets on all national and cross-national categories. New work based on local data gathering has been initiated for this purpose.

Symbols for missing data

Five symbols are employed in the tables and graphs to denote missing data:

a Data not applicable because the category does not apply.

m Data not available.

m: Data partially missing.

n Magnitude is either negligible or zero.

x Data included in another category/column of the table.

OECD member country codes

Australia	AUS	Italy	ITA
Austria	AUT	Japan	JPN
Belgium (Flemish Community)	BEL (Fl.)	Korea	KOR
Belgium (French Community)	BEL (Fr.)	Luxembourg	LUX
Canada Alberta	CAN (Alb.)	Mexico	MEX
Canada British Columbia	CAN (BC)	Netherlands	NLD
Canada New Brunswick	CAN (NB)	New Zealand	NZL
Canada Saskatchewan	CAN (SK)	Norway	NOR
Czech Republic	CZE	Poland	POL
Denmark	DNK	Portugal	PRT
Finland	FIN	Slovak Republic	SVK
France	FRA	Spain	ESP
Germany	DEU	Sweden	SWE
Greece	GRC	Switzerland	CHE
Hungary	HUN	Turkey	TUR
Iceland	ISL	United Kingdom (Eng.)	GBR
Ireland	IRL	United States	USA

Chapter 2
Analysis of the qualitative data

Background

This chapter analyses some qualitative descriptions provided by countries in addition to gathering quantitative data. These comprised:

- Information on the country's definition of special education used for gathering educational statistics.

- The use of categories in gathering data in this field along with the names and definitions of the categories and whether or not they fall within the resources definition.

- Whether there were categories of students currently used for data collection which fall within the resources definition but not within the national definition of special needs.

- How the categories fit into the cross-national categorisation A, B and C.

- How planning decisions are made to ensure that students with special educational needs receive appropriate additional resources.

- Whether there is specific coverage of special educational needs in the current legislative framework and if so what it is.

- Factors considered to be facilitators of inclusion and equity; and factors acting as barriers to inclusion and equity.

The following paragraphs synthesise the information that was provided in 1996, 1999 and 2001. Returns for the three years are collated from 28 OECD member countries: Austria, Belgium (Fl.), Canada (Alb., BC, NB, SK), the Czech Republic, Denmark, Finland, France, Germany, Greece, Hungary, Iceland, Ireland, Italy, Japan, Korea, Luxembourg, Mexico, the Netherlands, Norway, New Zealand, Poland, Portugal, Spain, Sweden, Switzerland, Turkey, the United Kingdom and the United States.

Laws

All countries surveyed have laws covering special education provision or the latter are in preparation or under review ensuring access to education for all students. Some are more specific than others. In the United Kingdom, for instance, a definition of learning difficulties is given in the Education Act (1976), whereas in contrast in the Czech Republic the laws are framed mainly in regard to provision for students with disabilities, difficulties and disadvantages, and the validity of Czech sign language for those with severe hearing disabilities. This latter situation is currently under review with the goal that special education will be included within the general framework of regular schools. Iceland, too, has no separate law for special education, which is covered in a sub-section of the general laws on education. Thus it is clear that this remains an area where there has been substantial development.

The most significant change in these legal frameworks is a move towards inclusion. This is being driven by an agenda comprising human rights issues, equity, parental involvement and social cohesion with the growing understanding that the concept of special educational needs implies that students' failures to make adequate progress in their learning are in large part the responsibility of the school and cannot be viewed as being caused wholly by the "disability" diagnosis.

The changes in thinking are reflected, for instance, in the Netherlands where new laws on Primary Education (WPO) and on special education (WEC) came into force in 1998. The WPO regulates primary education including the education of children attending special primary schools. According to the WPO, primary schools (including special primary schools) should offer all children appropriate instruction and an uninterrupted school career. All children should receive instruction geared to their educational needs, promoting intellectual, emotional growth and creativity and oriented to inclusion. Directly linked to this new funding system is a re-organisation of special education. The number of different special schools (now ten) will be reduced to four types of expertise centres for students with visual, communication, physical and mental disabilities and severe behaviour problems. Parallel arrangements for older students will come into force with a Secondary Education Act.

The interactive compensatory view of special educational needs has in some countries led to an expansion of the numbers of students under consideration to include those with disadvantages. In Denmark and Spain the term "special education requirements" is used and reflects the fact that many students will need a flexible approach to engender achievement. Furthermore, for instance in Mexico, it is importantly recognised that some disabled students may not have special educational needs. This follows from the observation that if certain disabilities are being skilfully handled in a school as part of the regular provision, additional help to access the curriculum is not needed.

The recognition that schools must adapt themselves is being reflected in other modifications to educational delivery. Where special needs students are included class sizes are sometimes reduced. In Hungary, for example, a student with special needs counts as two or three non-special needs students. So a class of 16, comprising two partially hearing students and 14 others would be equivalent to a class of 20 all non-special needs. More recent directives describe the necessary modifications and extensions to national core curriculum. To help regular schools adapt, outreach from special schools to regular schools is encouraged as is the development of clusters of schools. The aim here is to help develop the necessary skills in the regular schools so that those with special needs can be more effectively educated there. This approach has been described more fully elsewhere, *e.g.* in Canada (NB) (OECD, 1999).

Many countries also offer an extension in age of formal education for disabled students. In New Zealand this can extend from the under fives right up to the age of 21.

The significance of parental involvement is widely recognised especially in the assessment arrangements. But more and more parents are being given the right for their disabled child to be educated in regular schools as for instance in Italy (OECD, 1999).

How are planning decisions made to ensure that students with special educational needs receive appropriate additional resources?

Fifteen countries and four Canadian Provinces (Alb, BC, NB, and SK) responded to this question approaching the topic from many different viewpoints.

The majority of countries planned within the context of a national legal framework for identifying special needs students which included providing additional resources. This varied from the United States, whose complex federal system and federal laws require that States establish inter-agency agreements with agencies responsible for services for special education students, in contrast to Switzerland where there is no comprehensive uniform statutory approach.

Within these legal frameworks, special education students are identified and classified to varying degrees of complexity often via a multi-disciplinary approach, *e.g.* Luxembourg. These classifications form the basis for resource allocation. In Canada (Alb.) for instance, in 1999/2000, 9.88% of students were classified as having mild/moderate disabilities. To meet their special needs a particular sum is incorporated into the regular per capita student funding and school boards pool these resources to meet the needs of these students. In addition 2.58% of students are described as having severe disabilities, with each student receiving additional funding in addition to the regular per capita allowance. Other countries (*e.g.* Finland, the Netherlands) seem to have more complex arrangements but student classification remains the basis of subsequent statistical data gathering and planning. Resulting budgets could be determined for five year periods (*e.g.* the Netherlands) or annually (Mexico). Other countries such as Sweden appeared to have looser arrangements, frequently decentralised. In Germany, a qualitative and quantitative profile is demanded.

Countries varied considerably in the monitoring arrangements followed for ensuring that funds allotted for special education were used appropriately. In Canada (BC), for instance, there is a reporting and auditing process to ensure compliance. Schools themselves are also reviewed, and individual education plans for special needs students are required. This centralised process looks very different from the decentralised models that are working in countries such as Norway and Sweden. These countries appear to have less strong monitoring procedures in place and in the latter country there is a well used complaints procedure for parents who feel that their child is not receiving adequate support.

Methods were not uniformly applied across the cross-national categories A, B and C. For instance when students are in special schools (usually category A) resources are often based on actual numbers but if students are from disadvantaged backgrounds (category C) then determination of resources may be made on the basis of local indicators leading to block grants, such as in Italy and in funding education priority zones (ZEPs) in France. In the Netherlands resources needed for students from category A in regular schools are estimated from projections.

At the classroom level countries also varied in degree of specificity. For instance in Hungary in a classroom, one special needs student counts for two or three regular students in the calculation of class sizes. By contrast, in Canada (NB) the Superintendent must make sure that appropriate provision is made. Several countries make arrangements for students who cannot easily attend school to receive education at home and many extend the age-range outside the normal compulsory school age limits.

Facilitators and barriers of equity and inclusive education

Countries were asked to identify characteristics of their educational systems which they believe act as either facilitators or barriers to equity and inclusive education.

Given the diversity of systems involved it is not surprising that answers covered a wide range of topics from the legal system to the practicalities of assessment.

Legal frameworks

Many countries commented on the importance that legal and policy frameworks may play in encouraging inclusion and equity and creating respect for diversity or in creating barriers. Compulsory free education for all children and youth, and mandated integration in one country, were identified as obvious facilitators. If children are not in the system they can hardly be included! One identified the opportunities provided by the EU Helios programme on the inclusion of disabled students into mainstream schools as being especially helpful in achieving changes in attitudes and practices. In the United States (Individuals with Disabilities Education Act [IDEA] and the 1973 Rehabilitation Act) serve to guarantee education and the needed services in the least restrictive environment. In Greece, general educational reform and the development of new pedagogies and the implementation of new technologies were seen as beneficial for inclusion.

The monitoring of these laws for compliance was also given importance in some countries (*e.g.* Canada [BC]). In Italy the legal change of 1977 is credited with leading to a change in society stimulating a positive acceptance of disability where the school for instance is treated as a little community. In Switzerland, decentralisation of the educational system was also cited as a factor beneficial for inclusion. France noted that the central concept of education blocks individual treatment of students and the implementation of individual programme planning. Other countries noted that policies for inclusion were not always implemented consistently.

This relatively straightforward position may, however, be contrasted with other complex effects which appear when policies are put into practice. In Austria for instance, the abolition of statements of special needs for some students, guaranteeing certain forms of provision, were found to be a barrier to effective education of disabled students since without them they were obliged to follow the regular aims of the school. In addition, regular schools provided two years less required education than special schools. In contrast in the Flemish part of Belgium, the stigmatising effects of assessment and a heavy bureaucratic approach were identified as barriers to inclusion.

Educational structures

The historical structure of the education and special education systems were frequently cited as a severe barrier. These had led to inflexible school organisation (tracking for instance was viewed as a barrier to inclusion), over large class sizes, the lack of relevant teaching skills and of individualised teaching programmes, prejudiced attitudes on the part of teachers and parents, poor quality or limited teacher preparation, biased funding systems, unhelpful contractual agreements involving employers and trade-unions and a lack of co-operation between relevant ministries and services.

More recent developments in some countries such as the existence of pre-schools and special classes and special schools and a continuum of placement possibilities and links between special and mainstream schools were viewed as facilitators.

Funding

Funding of special education was also identified as a key factor. The creation of a level playing field for funding which does not bias placement decisions was seen as an important facilitator. In some countries, *e.g.* Denmark, Finland, Hungary and New Zealand, funds follow students and not schools and, at least in principle, this opens the way to inclusive practices. A paradox emerged in New Zealand with regard to the decentralisation of the special educational needs grant. While central control was viewed as a barrier to inclusion, and decentralisation seen as an important way to help local authorities implement relevant inclusionary policies, decentralisation in the form of the local management of schools in New Zealand was seen as a barrier. A general lack of funds and bias in funding formulae were both perceived to be barriers. Other countries, *e.g.* Switzerland and the United States, reported inconsistencies in the way funding formulae worked at local level while for others the lack of resources and the complexity of their delivery were viewed as barriers. Cuts in spending seemed to encourage segregated provision, partly perhaps because special schools were safeguarded but also because parents, perhaps for the same reason, thought that their children would receive higher quality provision there.

That resources are needed to develop inclusion and equity cannot be denied. Mexico for instance has modified buildings and provided free textbooks and materials aimed at DDD students. Furthermore, these have been translated for the indigenous communities and scholarships provided for students living in isolated areas. In Finland, nutrition and transport are arranged and in Canada (BC) extra funds are made available for in-service education (INSET) and a telephone help line. The government there has also made loans available for the purchase of expensive equipment.

Assessment and training

Many countries mentioned that assessment practices can both facilitate and block inclusion. In Sweden a change from a normative to a criterion-based model of pupil assessment led to more students with severe learning difficulties being identified as "failing" and this increased the likelihood of special school placement. In Canada (Alb.) annual tests with well planned accommodations were reported as facilitating inclusion while at the same time they were also seen as being a way of excluding students with difficulties from the testing arrangements. The reason given for this was fear on the part of schools that including students with special needs would lower average scores – an outcome challenged by research conducted in Alberta, which found just the opposite result.

In many countries, even for those who have been practising inclusion for many years, lack of training and skills was identified as main barrier. This appeared to hold at all levels of pre-service and in-service with a weakness in university level training being identified in one country, Canada (NB). The development of individual training programmes, preventive measures and early diagnosis were particularly mentioned. In Canada (SK), the degree of self-confidence of classroom teachers and school administrators was also cited in the face of growing pupil diversity and the need for more appropriate INSET and skill development. Class sizes were seen as a barrier to inclusion as was the need for effective support services, *e.g.* educational psychologists, speech/language pathologists, social workers and the use of classroom aides.

Others

Other aspects of structure were seen as barriers. These included a shorter period of education for regular students, in contrast to that available for those with disabilities, and the structure of primary education itself. At the classroom level, class size and streaming or tracking were seen as barriers. The lack of specialists and the proper use of teachers' aides were seen as obstacles to be overcome. On the positive side, the addition of extra teachers was a facilitator presumably because they bring additional skills to the classroom, allow for joint planning and lead to a reduction in pupil teacher ratio in classes where disabled students are included.

The involvement of parents as advocates facilitated inclusion but the lack of parental involvement and knowledge were viewed as barriers.

The existence of educational priority policy and non-discriminatory equal opportunities were also important in the fight for equity and deliberately balancing the numbers of ethnic minorities in schools was seen as a positive equity measure.

Definition of special education for gathering statistics

Based on the returns from the countries who responded to this question, the definition of special education for the purposes of gathering national statistics may be grouped into four basic patterns.

Almost all countries collect data via disability categories (always remembering that the term disability itself has limited common usage across countries and in France two systems, emanating from two ministries, operate in parallel); in Canada (SK), for instance, four criteria need to be met: a) the student needs to meet the classification criteria identified in the definitions; b) the student must be being provided with an appropriate programme that meets his/her needs; c) the programme must be delivered by, or the delivery must be supervised by, a teacher with special education teacher qualifications acceptable to the minister; and d) the costs of the programme are equal to or greater than the recognised costs in the grants structure.

Second, there are those countries such as Greece, Ireland and Switzerland, which also include disadvantaged students. Additionally, some countries such as Switzerland include children with a Foreign First Language within these categories whilst others do not.

Third, there are those, *e.g.* Canada (Alb., BC), Mexico, Spain and Turkey, which also include gifted students.

The fourth approach used in Denmark and in the United Kingdom[1] is to base provision on the need to respond to exceptionalities leading to perceived difficulties in the schooling process rather than defining students *per se* via a categorical approach.

The data are summarised in Table 2.1, which is provided at the end of this chapter.

Use of categories

The data show that most countries gather data by means of categories and this question invited them to provide the names of the categories and their definitions. Most countries were able to provide definitions and the outcomes are provided in full in Annex 1 which reveals the complexity of the different arrangements. In this annex the national categories have been placed into cross-national categories A, B and C according

---

1. This approach is no longer used in England. New data based on the current data collection method in that country will be reported in the next edition of this book.

to the classifications provided by the countries themselves as requested and as modified in subsequent discussions. Definitions of the categories are also provided where available. In addition, those categories which receive additional resources but which are not part of the national special needs category system are included in the table. A detailed discussion based on national categories is provided in Chapter 3.

Some countries report having categories which receive additional resources but which lie outside their national definition of special needs. These tend to cover disadvantaged students, those from ethnic minorities and those with short term learning problems and those with specific learning difficulties. However, some countries include gifted students, those with mild behaviour problems and those with speech impairments. These categories of provision exist in other countries too, but in those countries they will be included under the general rubric of special education.

A small number of countries do not fit this classification and fit into the fourth pattern noted above. This approach deserves further comment. The Canadian Province of New Brunswick does not keep categorical data but does have categories which receive resources but are not part of the special needs framework. The United Kingdom does not gather data by categories but for the current data round was able to identify students with special needs but without statements who received extra resources. These were placed in cross-national category B. Denmark also has a non-categorical system but makes a distinction between students with more extensive special needs (being about 1% who have the most severe disabilities and who need extensive support with their learning) and those with less extensive needs (being about 12% and including those with disadvantages); a framework which is conceptually similar to that in the United Kingdom where 2.74% of students with special education needs have statements of special educational need and a further 14.41% have special educational needs but do not have statements in compulsory education. Resourcing arrangements for these two groups are different. In these three countries resources are made available for the increased costs which arise in educating students with special educational needs, but they are allotted through local decision-making structures.

Cross-national classification

Countries were asked to carry out the task of re-classifying their categories both national and resource-based according to the cross-national model described in Chapter 1.

The allotment of national categories to cross-national categories was verified at the meetings of participating countries and the results are summarised in Table 2.2 which includes category definitions.

Table 2.2 reveals that the majority of countries use categories to classify their special needs population for the purposes of statistical data gathering. In terms of national categories, *i.e.* excluding those that additionally fall into the resources definition, they vary between two, *e.g.* the United Kingdom (Eng.), and 19 in Switzerland. Between these extremes many countries use 12 or 13. Although the categories used cover broadly similar disabling conditions, in many countries actual definitions in use render comparisons difficult. For instance, in regard to students with learning difficulties as far as cross-national comparisons are concerned, it is not possible to distinguish between students who would appear under the various headings of severe learning difficulties, moderate learning difficulties, light learning difficulties and learning disabilities. Some countries gather data on students who are blind or have visual impairment separately, others group them together, and similarly for those with serious or partial hearing impairments.

Students with emotional and behavioural problems represent an interesting case. In Greece, Hungary, Italy and Turkey there is no such category.

The increased availability of detailed definitions for most national categories has increased the reliability of their allocation to cross-national categories A, B and C, since the understanding of the wide variety of national category names is facilitated. However, some anomalies remained, and this has led to the need to re-allocate some national categories.

The main proposed reallocation was of "mild mental handicap" (and equivalently named categories) from cross-national category B to A. This was mainly because, while some countries have a separate "mild mental handicap" category which was placed in B, others have wider categories including both mild and more severe mental handicap, currently allocated to A. Placing all mental handicap (and equivalently named categories) in cross-national category A removes the inconsistency.

A similar reallocation of "children suffering from protracted illnesses', "health impaired" (and equivalently named categories) from B to A has been agreed. During earlier allocations, while B was a residual category, there was some justification for allocating these students to B (in that these categories are somewhat different from the typical categories currently in A). Their reallocation helps in framing a coherent substantive definition for B.

This discussion of the results of the findings on national categories and the way they are allotted to the cross-national categories of A, B and C strongly supports the rationale of the present study. That is, if meaningful international comparisons are to be made, a method such as the one developed here, which includes all children receiving additional resources and their allotment into straightforward and operationally defined categories, substantially simplifies the situation and improves the possibility of making policy relevant decisions based on internationally valid comparisons.

Concluding comments

In general terms the qualitative data gathered during the study reveals the great national interest in this area as laws, policies and educational provision are adjusted to meet the needs of students who are failing in the regular system. Factors thought to be facilitators for, or barriers to equity and inclusion, cover a whole range of issues which include legal frameworks, funding models, assessment arrangements, school structure, class size, individual teaching programmes, involvement of additional teachers and aides, teacher training, parental involvement and co-operation with other services. Together these make a substantial agenda for reform.

The quantitative data gathered by means of the electronic questionnaire will be examined in detail within the next three chapters.

Table 2.1. **Classification of nationally gathered categories used in collecting data within the national definition of special educational needs[1]**

PATTERNS / COUNTRIES	Disability categories only	Disability categories plus disadvantaged students	Disability categories plus gifted and talented students	Essentially non categorical systems
Austria	✓			
Belgium (Fl.)	✓			
Belgium (Fr.)	✓			
Canada (Alb.)			✓	
Canada (BC)			✓	
Canada (NB)	✓			
Canada (SK)	✓			
Czech Republic		✓		
Denmark				✓
Finland	✓			
France	✓			
Germany	✓			
Greece		✓[2]		
Hungary	✓			
Italy	✓			
Ireland		✓[2]		
Japan		✓[2]		
Korea	✓			
Luxembourg	✓			
Mexico			✓	
Netherlands	✓			
New Zealand		✓		
Norway				✓
Poland		✓		
Portugal	✓			
Slovak Republic		✓		
Spain			✓[3]	
Sweden		✓		
Switzerland		✓[2]		
Turkey			✓[3]	
United Kingdom (Eng.)				✓
United States	✓			

1. This table combines 1996, 1999 and 2001 data.
2. Includes learning difficulties linked to linguistic barriers or disadvantage associated with ethnic groupings.
3. Includes disadvantaged students.

Table 2.2. **Allocation of categories of students with disabilities, difficulties and disadvantages included in the resources definition to cross-national categories A, B and C**

Belgium (Flemish Community)

Cross-national category A

1. Minor mental handicap – Type 1. Education in type 1 of special education is organised for children with mild mental disabilities: they should be able to acquire basic school knowledge and skills; and to receive vocational training in order to make integration in the regular social and professional environment possible. This type of education is not organised in nursery school (*i.e.* this type of education is only organised at primary and secondary school level).

2. Moderate or serious mental handicap – Type 2. Education in type 2 of special education is organised for children with moderate to severe mental disabilities. Through social education and special vocational training, children with moderate mental disabilities are prepared for integration in a protected socio-professional environment. The social self-reliance level of children with severe mental disabilities is enhanced by special educational activities. This type of education is organised at pre-primary, primary and secondary level.

4. Pupils with a physical handicap – Type 4. This category covers pupils with a physical handicap. Education in type 4 of special education is organised to fulfil the educational needs of children with physical disabilities, other than those mentioned in types 5, 6 and 7, who are not able to receive education in a standard school because they regularly need medical or paramedical treatments and/or special teaching materials. This type of education is organised at pre-primary, primary and secondary level.

5. Children suffering from protracted illness – Type 5. This category covers pupils suffering from protracted illness. Education in type 5 of special education is organised to fulfil the educational needs of children who suffer from an illness and receive medical treatment in a hospital or in a medical-pedagogical institute organised or accredited by the State. This type of education is organised at pre-primary, primary and secondary level.

6. Visual handicap – Type 6. This category covers pupils with a visual handicap. Education in type 6 of special education is organised for blind or visually-impaired children who regularly need medical or paramedical treatment and/or special teaching materials. This type of education is organised at pre-primary, primary and secondary level.

7. Auditory handicap – Type 7. This type of special education is for pupils with an auditory handicap. Education in type 7 of special education is organised for deaf or hearing-impaired children who regularly need medical or paramedical treatment and/or special teaching materials. This type of education is organised at pre-primary, primary and secondary level.

9. Support at home for children who are temporarily ill. Temporary home-based education applies to both ordinary and special primary education (except for type 5 schools). A child of compulsory school age in primary school (not in nursery education) has the right to receive temporary home-based education when the following conditions are simultaneously satisfied: an absence of over 21 calendar days caused by an illness or an accident; the parents have submitted a written request, accompanied by a medical certificate, to the principal of the school providing home-based education. The medical certificate should show that the child is not able to come to the school but is allowed to be educated; the distance between the school site and the pupil's residence should not exceed 10 km for ordinary education or 20 km for special education. The home-based education is provided from the 22nd calendar day of absence and continues until the child is able to return to its regular school. If the child should suffer from the same illness or accident within three months, the 21-day waiting period does not apply. In order to organise the home-based education, four additional teaching periods per week and per pupil are financed or granted. The travel expenses incurred by the staff member providing the home-based education are repaid according to the value of a first-class train ticket.

Pupils in permanent home-based education are also included in this category. Pupils at compulsory school age who satisfy the admission requirements for special primary education but for whom it is permanently impossible to be educated in a school due to a handicap, are entitled to permanent home-based education. This does require a recommendation from the Special Education Advisory Committee. Great distance to a school, long transport time, etc., do not qualify as reasons for applying for permanent home-based education. The deciding factor is the seriousness of the handicap which does not allow education in a school, although the child is able to receive education. The school receives four additional teaching periods per week to organise the permanent home-based education. These additional teaching periods are to be performed by a member of the teaching staff and they can never contain any therapeutic treatments.

Cross-national category B
3. Serious emotional and/or behavioural problems – Type 3. This category covers pupils with serious emotional and/or behavioural problems. Education in type 3 of special education is organised for children with personality disorders. They suffer from severe structural and/or functional disorders in the affective-dynamic and relational aspect of their personality, which make special educational and psycho-therapist measures necessary. This type of education is organised at pre-primary, primary and secondary level.

8. Serious learning disabilities – Type 8. This type of special education is organised for pupils with serious learning disabilities. Education in type 8 of special education is organised to fulfil the educational needs of children with severe learning disabilities. Although their mental, visual and hearing abilities are normal, they suffer from disorders in their development of language and skills of speech, reading, writing and/or arithmetic. This type of education is only organised at primary school level (not for nursery school or secondary education).

11. Remedial teaching. Remedial teachers in ordinary primary education. The total of teaching periods in primary education is conceived in such a way that primary schools have the opportunity to devote special attention and care to children with learning or developmental difficulties. One of the most important goals of giving the schools this autonomy is to make sure that schools are organised so that remediation is possible. In primary education, pedagogical reform is ensured by working with differentiation elements, carrying out different groupings and taking maximum advantage of remedial teachers. In addition, a lot of attention is paid to consultative conversations between the regular teachers and the remedial teacher, and between the regular teachers, the remedial teacher, the members of the Pupil Guidance Centre, and the school principal. One teaching period for the remedial teacher per group of 20 pupils seems a minimum. It is the remedial teacher's task to help children with learning or developmental difficulties and to detect barriers to learning. The guidance takes place individually or in small groups or assistance within the regular classroom, according to the pupils' needs. The remedial teacher's presence is not based on additional teaching periods or allowances, but is made possible by the flexible allocation of the total number of teaching periods that is assigned to each school based on the total number of pupils. This total package of granted teaching periods is called *omkadering*.

Cross-national category C
10. Extending care. For a few years now, the Flemish Government has been developing a programme for *zorgbreedte* (extending care). It is rather difficult to translate this notion. The idea is linked up with ideas on, for example, "inclusive education". The idea is to organise early attention for those children who might suffer from learning difficulties that may cause problems in the transition between pre-school and primary school. Additional teachers, schools for special education and the pupil guidance centre (CLB) work closely together with the pre-school teacher. Attention is given to general language proficiency, social skills, prevention and remediation of learning difficulties, socio-emotional problems and co-operation with the parents. The target group consists of children who live in less favourable economic and cultural circumstances but who are capable of participating in ordinary education when certain deficits are eliminated.

12. Educational priority policy. The languages of the migrant population are not legally recognised as minority languages. Nevertheless, a special policy has been instituted within the education system to provide for adequate learning opportunities, especially for children within compulsory education. This policy is called the *onderwijsvoorrangsbeleid* (educational priority policy). This policy is applied at the primary and secondary levels in schools with a significant number of migrant or refugee children. Schools must develop an educational approach with special attention to the quality of the teaching of Dutch intercultural education, the tackling of learning and developmental problems and co-operation with the immigrant families.

13. Reception classes for pupils who do not speak Dutch. Reception education is education for immigrant school entrants who do not speak Dutch and this is to develop their knowledge of Dutch and to facilitate their social integration. After this reception education, the pupils can enrol in regular education (primary or secondary school level). Reception education encourages the active integration of the immigrant school entrant in school life. The focus is on the relationship with the teachers and the other pupils of his/her peer group. In elementary education, schools with at least four foreign pupils who do not speak Dutch (*anderstalige nieuwkomers*) and who do not fully understand the language used at school may organise a special language adaptation course for three periods a week. In secondary education, this type of education is organised in 29 selected schools which have at least ten foreign pupils who do not speak Dutch.

14. Travelling children. In this category, two specific smaller projects are integrated. The first project concerns the reception of pre-school children of travelling employed population (circus, bargemen, fairmen, showmen, etc.). In the second project, three elementary schools take care of the reception of gypsy children.

15. Children placed in a sheltered home by juvenile court. These children are placed in a sheltered home by juvenile courts and this due to family problems. These children are integrated into regular schools. They are counted as 1.5 (instead of 1) to determine the yearly amount of teaching periods for the school.

16. More favourable teacher/pupil ratio in the schools of the Capital region of Brussels. Because of the cultural and linguistic differences of pupils going to school in the Capital region of Brussels (a lot of them do not speak Dutch), a more favourable teacher/pupil ratio is used in comparison to schools in Flanders.

17. Additional resources for schools in some municipalities around the Capital region of Brussels and at the linguistic border between the Flemish and the Walloon regions. In six municipalities around the Capital region of Brussels and the linguistic border between the Flemish and the Walloon regions, schools can receive additional resources. These additional resources are project-based (based on a work plan for the pupils with cultural and linguistic differences).

Belgium (French Community)

Cross-national category A

1. Mild mental retardation – Type 1. Type 1 of special needs teaching is organised at the primary and secondary level for students with mild mental retardation: they receive basic education and technical and vocational education allowing integration in a social and professional environment.

2. Moderate or profound mental retardation – Type 2. Type 2 of special needs teaching concerns children with moderate or profound mental retardation. Depending on the level of the handicap, it is a matter of preparing the students to integrate a protected socio-professional environment or to occupy them with specific activities. This type is organised at the pre-primary, primary and secondary levels.

4. Physical deficiencies – Type 4. Type 4 special needs teaching is attended by students with physical handicaps. These students cannot attend regular classes because of these medical, paramedical or material needs. This type is organised at the pre-primary, primary and secondary levels.

5. Students suffering from an illness – Type 5. This type enables children suffering from an illness who are in a hospital or a medicopedagogic institute to continue their schooling. This type exists at the kindergarten, primary and secondary levels.

6. Visual deficiencies – Type 6. This type is organised at the pre-primary, primary and secondary levels.

7. Hearing impairment – Type 7. This type exists at the pre-primary, primary and secondary levels.

Cross-national category B

3. Character and/or personality disorders. Level 3 of special needs teaching is organised at the pre-primary, primary and secondary levels.

8. Instrumental disorders – Type 8. This type is only organised at the primary level for students with learning disabilities concerning language, reading, writing and/or counting.

Cross-national category C

9. Children placed by judges or under the jurisdiction of juvenile courts. The children are placed in a home by juvenile courts because of problems in their family. They are schooled in normal institutions.

10. Children attending positive discrimination schools. The difficulties in a social or school environment of the children as well as the framework for support in the schools have led policy makers to launch a programme of "positive discrimination". It consists in effect of voluntary actions, aiming in the name of solidarity, at giving more to those who have less, based on the principle that it is unequal to treat very different situations in the same way. It is a matter of distinguishing the institutions with a proportion of students living in areas presenting, in objective statements, standards of living that are inferior to national averages with regards to socio-economic typology. The selected institutions must promote educational actions aiming at giving all students equal chances for social emancipation. Each institution benefiting from positive discrimination policies receives additional human and material resources.

11. New arrivals in schools. Children aged from 2.5 to 18 can benefit from new provision created by the decree of June 2001, when they received stateless or refugee determination, or already had it, being nationals of certain developing countries, or having arrived in the country less than a year before. These students go into "bridge" classes for periods varying from one week to six months, not exceeding a one-year period during which they will benefit from a specific teaching framework enabling them to adapt to the socio-economic and school systems of the country and to be directed towards the level and orientation which will be best for them.

12. Differentiated teaching for rural areas. Schools located in rural areas with few inhabitants and far from a similar institution will have more teachers (with regards to the number of students) in secondary education.

Canada – New Brunswick (District 18)

Cross-national category A

2. Communicational. Students who require support because of deficits in speech/articulation development and language.

3. Intellectual. Students who may require modified or long term intensive special educational programmes or services to develop their academic and social potential.

4. Physical. Medical/health; physically handicapped students who, because of physically challenging conditions, require mobility assistance or adaptation to the physical environment and/or personal care. These include hearing and visually impaired students who received services from APSEA (Atlantic Provinces Special Education Authority).

5. Perceptual. Students who because of specific learning disabilities continue to experience a wide range of difficulties in coping in the regular classroom environment.

6. Multiple. Students who have combinations of challenging disabilities.

<u>**Cross-national category B**</u>
1. Behavioural exceptionalities. Students with severe behavioural challenges that are primarily a result of social, psychological and environmental factors.

<u>**Cross-national category C**</u>
7. Immigrant. Students who receive tutorial funding to acquire skills in English language.

Czech Republic

<u>**Cross-national category A**</u>
1. Mentally retarded. All students in the educational system with mental handicaps (in special schools, special classes, regular schools) who need modified education or special educational plans. Also included here are profoundly mentally retarded children in auxiliary schools, who receive a specially adapted education.
2. Hearing handicaps. Students with hearing handicaps – deaf, partially hearing, etc. – who need special education (in special schools, special classes, regular schools).
3. Sight handicaps. Students with sight handicaps – blind, partially sighted, etc. – who need special education (in special schools, special classes, regular schools).
4. Speech handicaps. Students with speech handicaps who need special education (in special schools, special classes, regular schools).
5. Physical handicaps. Students with all physical handicaps who need special education (in special schools, special classes, regular schools).
6. Multiple handicaps. Students with all combinations of handicaps who need special education.
7. Hospitalised students. Hospitalised students (and those attending school in hospitals), students in medical institutions.
9. Other handicaps. All other handicapped children (which are not defined in the other categories).
10. With weakened health (kindergarten only). Children with weakened health in kindergartens, which need special educational approach.
12. Autistic. Autistic children and students (in special schools, special classes, regular classes).

<u>**Cross-national category B**</u>
8. Development, behaviour and learning problems. Students with all development, behaviour and learning problems (including dysgraphia, dyslexic children, etc.), which need special educational approach.

<u>**Cross-national category C**</u>
11. Social disadvantaged children, preparatory classes in regular schools. Children in special classes for social disadvantaged children in regular schools, students from reformatory educational institution for children and youth.

Finland

<u>**Cross-national category A**</u>
1. Mild mental impairment (MIMI). Education of pupils needing adjustment of curriculum and extra support (education for students with mild mental impairment). Adjustment may concern all or only some subjects. Pupils have been transferred to special needs education and IEP (Individual Education Plan) has to be drawn up for them.

2. Moderate mental impairment (MOMI). Education of mentally disabled students needing adjustment of curriculum and extensive support. Pupils have been transferred to special needs education and IEP has to be drawn up for them.

3. Most severe mental impairment (SMI). Education of pupils with the most severe mental impairment needing extensive support and curriculum is based on training of everyday activities. The most severely mentally handicapped pupils follow a curriculum with five function areas which are motor skills, language and communication, social skills, daily living skills and cognitive skills. Pupils have been transferred to special needs education and IEP has to be drawn up for them.

4. Hearing impairment (HI). Education of the hearing-impaired. Includes deaf and partially hearing pupils, who have been transferred to special needs education and IEP has to be drawn up for them.

5. Visual impairment (VI). Education of the visually impaired. Includes blind and partially sighted pupils, who have been transferred to special needs education and IEP has to be drawn up for them.

6. Physical & other impairment (POHI). Education of the disabled (physical disabilities, neurological disabilities, developmental disorders). Pupils have been transferred to special needs education and IEP has to be drawn up for them.

8. Other impairment. Education of pupils with metabolic or nutritional disorders, including abnormal development and maturation, gluten intolerance, diabetes, epilepsy, malnutrition or other impairments which are not defined in other categories. Education of pupils, who are being treated in clinics or hospitals and who are capable of taking part in lessons as well as pupils with chronic illnesses, who cannot therefore take part in regular instruction. Education according to the general education curriculum, or pupils have been transferred to special needs education and IEP has to be drawn up for them.

<u>Cross-national category B</u>
7. Emotional or social impairment (EI). Education of the maladjusted. Pupils have serious emotional and/or behavioral problems and they have been transferred to special needs education and IEP has to be drawn up for them.

9. Speech difficulties. Part-time special needs education of students with speech difficulties. Pupils have problems in articulation, fluency, voice and verbalization and there are difficulties in communication and learning. Students belonging to this category follow the regular curriculum.

10. Reading and writing difficulties. Part-time special needs education of students with reading and writing difficulties. Students belonging to this category follow the regular curriculum.

11. Speech, reading and writing difficulties. Part-time special needs education of students with speech, reading and writing difficulties. Students belonging to this category follow the regular curriculum.

12. Learning difficulties in mathematics. Part-time special needs education aiming at relieving learning difficulties in mathemathics. Students belonging to this category follow the regular curriculum.

13. Learning difficulties in foreign languages. Part-time special needs education aiming at relieving learning difficulties in foreign languages. Students belonging to this category follow the regular curriculum.

14. General learning difficulties. Part-time special needs education aiming at relieving general learning difficulties. Students belonging to this category follow the regular curriculum.

15. Emotional and social difficulties. Part-time special needs education for the maladjusted. Children and youth with behavioural and conduct difficulties and/or emotional difficulties. Students belonging to this category follow the regular curriculum.

16. Other special difficulties. Part-time special needs education for difficulties, which are not defined in other categories. Students belonging to this category follow the regular curriculum.

18. Remedial teaching. Temporary, part-time teaching usually provided by a general education teacher for students who have temporarily fallen behind in their studies or who need other special support. Students belonging to this category follow the regular curriculum.

<u>**Cross-national category C**</u>
17. Immigrants' remedial teaching. Periodic, part-time remedial teaching for students who have moved to Finland from abroad; mother tongue teaching for Sámi, Romany and foreign-language speakers; and teaching for Finnish students who have moved back to Finland from abroad in order to maintain the language skills they have acquired abroad. Students belonging to this category follow the regular curriculum.

France

<u>**Cross-national category A**</u>
1. Severe mental handicap. Severe mental handicap (IQ between 20 & 34) concerns persons who can benefit from the systematic learning of simple gestures.
2. Moderate mental handicap. Moderate mental handicap (IQ between 35 & 49) concerns persons able to acquire simple notions of communication, hygiene and elementary safety as well as simple manual skills, but who are incapable of learning how to do arithmetic or reading.
3. Mild mental handicap. This category covers handicaps as regards intelligence, memory and thinking. It concerns persons (IQ between 50 & 70) capable of learning practical skills and how to read, as well as notions of arithmetic thanks to special education, and who can be taught a certain degree of socialisation.
4. Physical handicap. Orthopaedic and motor deficiencies have been broadly interpreted as covering the structure of the body and its visible parts. Such handicaps include mechanical and functional alterations to the face, head, neck, trunk and limbs, as well as limbs which are missing in whole or in part.
5. Metabolic disorders. Metabolic or nutritional disorders include abnormal development and maturation, gluten intolerance, diabetes, malnutrition, and weight loss or gain (but exclude thinness and obesity).
6. Deaf. Disorders in this category concern not only the ear but also its ancillary parts and its functions. The most important sub-division is that of hearing impairment. The term "deaf" should only be applied to persons whose hearing impairment is such that it cannot be helped by any hearing aid. Like blindness, deafness is a serious sensory impairment.
7. Partially hearing. Disorders in this category concern not only the ear but also its ancillary parts and functions. The most important sub-division is that of hearing impairment.
8. Blind. Blindness is a serious sensory impairment. Such impairment may be marked (very poor vision or partial blindness), almost total (severe or almost total blindness) or total (no perception of light). It may affect one eye or both.
9. Partially sighted. Other visual impairments include astigmatism, accommodation deficiency, diplopia (strabismus), amblyopia, and sensitivity to light.
10. Other neuropsychological disorders. Neuropsychological disorders have been defined to include any interference with the basic elements of the mental process. This being so, the functions listed are those which normally involve the presence of basic neuropsychological and psychological mechanisms.
11. Speech and language disorders. Speech disorders or impairment include artificial larynx, severe dysarthria, lack of voice expression, and stuttering; while language disorders or impairment include central impairment of the visual function with inability to communicate (*e.g.* severe dyslexia).
12. Other deficiencies. Other deficiencies are all those not mentioned above.
13. Multiply handicapped. Children or young people in special educational establishments suffer from a main handicap, which is usually the reason they are attending special classes. But they may suffer from other disorders in addition to this main one.

Cross-national category B

15. Learning difficulties. Special 3rd year classes and 4th year vestibule classes (second level) provide assistance and support to pupils with problems at school and unable to derive benefit from the general and technical instruction normally given. Together with remedial classes, they form part of the system of assistance, support and insertion. SEGPAs (special sections for general or occupational training) are incorporated into public and private secondary schools (usually lower secondary ones). They make it easier for pupils with learning difficulties to pursue their studies.

Cross-national category C

14. Non-francophone students. Initiation classes (CLINs) have been created in primary schools for non-French speaking pupils of foreign nationality. Reception classes, in 1st to 4th year secondary (but mainly 1st year), are offered to foreign pupils (in principle, non-French speaking, newly arrived in France and whose age corresponds to that of the school).

16. Disadvantaged children – ZEP. "Education Priority Areas" (Zones d'éducation prioritaires [ZEP]) are geographical surfaces – communes, districts – in which a policy of differentiated education is essential. Two types of criteria governed the delimitation of these underprivileged surfaces: first – school (rate of redoubling, density in vocational schools, classes of reception, etc.); second – socio-economic (low level of study of the parents, poverty, unemployment, discomfort of the dwellings, maladjustment to the language or the culture). ZEPs are also and especially a community project of development centred on the school and aiming at making the children of popular medium fully enjoy their rights to education.

Germany

Cross-national category A

2. Partially sighted or blind. Students: 1) having a central visual acuity in the better eye or in both eyes of 0.3 or less for distance despite a correction by glasses but without other aids; or 2) having a visual acuity of 0.3 (Nieden V) or less for the proximity regarding a working distance of at least 30 centimetres; or 3) whose faculty of vision is impaired to a similar degree despite better visual acuity; or 4) blind children or youths without visual faculty or whose visual faculty is largely impaired resulting in an inability to act like seeing persons (even after an optical correction, *e.g.* glasses).

3. Partially hearing or deaf. Children or youth who suffer a loss of hearing of more than 90 db in the frequency range above 500 cps or whose hearing is affected in such way that even with hearing aids they need special education; or deaf students who, irrespective of their actual deficiency in hearing capacity, are not capable of noticing acoustic signals of their environment and to make use of them for acquiring speech, speech hearing and an active or phonetic speech competence.

4. Speech impairment. Children or youth whose speech and development of speaking is largely impaired because of: 1) marked under development of speech with symptoms of multiple or universal stammering and/or grammar; 2) disorders in trained speech required at an early stage (aphasia, dysphasia); 3) central handicaps in speech development (audimutismus, acute agnosia); 4) morbid changes in the speech organs so that entry into or staying in a regular school with ambulant school-accompanying promotion programmes is regarded as insufficient.

5. Physically handicapped. Children or youth with cerebral motor disturbances, myopathia, malformations, paraplegia and other resulting in disorders, retardations, deficits in locomotion and other disabilities which implies the need for special education and further measures and facilities.

6. Mentally handicapped. Children or youth who are severely mentally disabled as a result of damage to the central nervous system before or after birth and who have conspicuous peculiarities in their cognitive and emotional absorption and storage processes, expressive behaviour, motor abilities and their verbal and non-verbal communication.

8. Sick. Children who are being treated in clinics, hospitals or sanatoriums for a longer period of time and who are capable of taking part in lessons as well as students with chronic illnesses who cannot therefore take part in regular instructions.

9. Multiple handicaps. Children and youth with more than one handicap to be taken into account in the development of learning.

12. Autism. Children and youth with a severe developmental disability in verbal and non-verbal communication and social interaction with resistance to environmental changes and mostly engaged in repetitive activities and stereotyped movements – based on complex impairment of the central nervous system. (No statistical data of the large groups available, but programmes are provided.)

<u>**Cross-national category B**</u>

1. Learning disability. Children or youth needing promotion through special education due to a severe extensive and long lasting deficiency in learning development, in thinking, remembering, using language, perception, movement, emotion and interaction. The relation between self and environment is permanently difficult. Aims and contents of the mainstream curricula cannot be fulfilled.

7. Behavioural disorders. Children or youth with behavioural and conduct disorders and/or emotional disorders who need special education to learn from appropriate experiences and develop social competences.

10. Special needs in pre-primary education. Pre-school classes for five-year-old children with special educational needs who have not yet reached compulsory school age but whose parents wish that they receive assistance in their preparation for primary school. Attendance is voluntary.

11. Diagnostic and support classes. Special classes to observe children with special educational needs at the beginning of the attendance of special schools to promote them and to integrate these children in the most appropriate category of special education needs.

13. Remedial instruction. Students with need of support because of particular and limited difficulties in basic skill concerning reading, writing or numeracy. (No statistical data of the large groups available, but programmes are provided.)

<u>**Cross-national category C**</u>

14. Travelling families. Children and youth with need of support because their parents are itinerant workers (circus, fairs, barges). (No statistical data of the large groups available, but programmes are provided.)

15. German for speakers of other languages. Children and youth with need of support because they do not have appropriate competence in German, so that they cannot follow the instruction with adequate effects and success. (No statistical data of the large groups available, but programmes are provided.)

Greece

<u>**Cross-national category A**</u>

1. Visual impairments. According to the Law of Special Education 2817/14-03-2000 students maybe called blind, amblyope or partially sighted, if they have serious problems in vision. The term "blind" refers to students who learn via Braille or other non-visual media. The term "partially sighted" refers to students who require adaptation in lighting or the size of print in order to learn through reading.

The Greek educational system insists that students use their residual vision so that the sensory motor abilities may be reinforced. Delays or losses in orientation, mobility, communication, cognitive, and/or social development may be prevented.

Blind students attend special education schools at primary level and mainstream schools for secondary education. There is no differentiation for partially sighted students. Blind and partially sighted students follow the general educational curricula. The Ministry of Education develops special measures in order to meet the needs of the blind.

2. Hearing impairments. The term "deaf" refers to students who are severely impaired in processing linguistic information through hearing, with or without amplification. The term "hearing impaired" refers to students whose impairment in hearing, whether permanent or fluctuating, affects the educational performance. Thus, deafness prevents an individual from receiving sound in all or most of its forms. In contrast, a child with a hearing loss can generally respond to auditory stimuli, including speech.

The distinction between deaf and hearing impaired is indispensable for diagnosis. The ability to learn oral skills depends in large part on the degree of hearing impairment. It also depends on the age at which the student became deaf (especially whether it was before or after acquiring spoken language), the timing of diagnosis of the impairment, the onset of early intervention, the family and the educational system.

The Law of Special Education (2817/2000, Article 2: Organisation) stresses the importance of early diagnosis. A team consisting of a primary school teacher, a secondary school teacher, one psychologist, one social worker and an administrative officer serves at each Centre for Diagnosis, Assessment and Pedagogical Support all over the country. Some centres are additionally staffed with specialists such as a pre-school teacher, a speech therapist, a child psychologist, an audiologist and a sign language specialist. These centres are called KDAY.

Deaf students follow the common core curricula, which are appropriately adapted to meet their needs with emphasis given on spoken language and on articulation. The national educational system provides students with equal opportunities for education and vocational training and promotes social integration. Deaf and partially hearing students attend special education schools (pre-school, primary and secondary) as well as special classes at secondary education.

3. Physical impairments. This category refers to students with serious neurological problems or orthopaedic disabilities within a heterogeneous grouping of conditions with a wide range of causes. Examples of some of the more common causes are: nervous system disorders, traumatic spinal cord injury, muscular dystrophy, cerebral palsy, epilepsy, muscular-skeletal disorders, cardiovascular disease, coronary heart disease, respiratory disorders, emphysema, asthma, endocrine-metabolic, diabetes and amputations of all types.

Students with motor disabilities may attend special education schools or mainstream school units. They are taught the same national curricula at primary and secondary level from the age of 6 to 22. After completing the compulsory education, students may follow studies at: a) general upper secondary level schools from 14 to 22 of age (Lykeio); b) technical professional schools (T.E.E.) of special education either during the compulsory education (A' level), or after the general compulsory education (B' level); c) laboratories of special professional education from 14 to 22, according to article 2 of the Law 2640/1998. Teachers of students at primary level receive a two-year training course whereas the Ministry of Education and Religious Affairs has recently designed training programmes on special education for secondary education teachers, which are being implemented by universities within the Operational Plan "Education and Initial Vocational Training" of the 2nd European Community Support Framework.

4. Mental impairments. This category refers to students who have mental impairments, incompetence or immaturity. The term mental impairments vary considerably. It may define mental retardation; *i.e.* significantly sub-average general intellectual functioning, existing concurrently with deficits in adaptive behaviour, and manifested during the developmental period that adversely affects a child's educational performance. Difficulties may occur in communication, in social, academic, vocational, and independent living skills. A child may develop slowly without being mentally retarded or it may be retarded without slow development being present. Mental retardation can be assigned if there are procedures and tests related to the type of retardation and if the genetic conditions and the environmental hazards are in any case examined.

According to 603/82 presidential decrees, an individual is diagnosed and classified as having mental retardation by a qualified team of doctors and educators and by prefectural committees. The team gives one or more standardised (intelligence and adaptive skills) tests, on an individual basis. The test results determine the educational setting that is most appropriate for the student. Students with mental impairments are characterised by the team as educable (I.Q. 50-70), trainable (I.Q. 30-50) and profoundly retarded (I.Q. under 30). According to the diagnosis, the Ministry of Education classifies the students to the appropriate school unit.

5. Autism. According to the law 2817/14-03-2002, Article 1, autism has been included in a general category which comprises emotional and social difficulties as well as developmental disorders. Autistic children may present profound or less severe difficulties in behaviour. Development may present unsteadiness unlike mental retardation that can have slower but steadier improvement. According to this law children with autism are not categorised as handicapped. The new law introduced considerable changes in the framework of special education, one of them being the inclusion of autism as a special educational difficulty. Children with autism are under the supervision of the Ministry of Health and Welfare and are educated at special institutions. More and more children are being admitted in Special Education Schools of the Ministry of Education where there is provision in the form of special educational programmes.

This policy signals an effort to prevent children with autism from being institutionalised, and include them in primary education. The goals (academic and non-academic) and objectives of the educational programmes may include social skills, functional skills (dressing, toilet training, feeding oneself, etc.), communication, and behaviour modification. From 1998, teachers are being trained in the special educational needs of autism within the Operational Plan "Education and Initial Vocational Training" of the 2nd European Community Support Framework.

7. Multiple impairments. This category includes students studying in special schools in some regions of the country. Students happen to present hearing, visual or sensory-motor educational needs but it is not possible for them to follow the special school for their category. This is the case of some regions in remote areas. Students cannot leave their homes and the state educational system establishes a special school unit in which support is provided according to the particular need of the child. Students of category 8 may also be met in this category of special schools in remote areas of the country.

Cross-national category B
6. Learning difficulties. Students with learning difficulties are described as "having difficulties in learning, *i.e.* dyslexia, dyscalculia, difficulties in reading" (Law 2817/14-03-2000, art.1, e.). By learning difficulties we refer to difficulties due to various reasons and factors: pathological, psychological, unfavourable school environment. This umbrella category covers several sub-categories of learning difficulties which often are combined with autism and/or mental impairments, behaviour disturbances, communication disorders, emotional disturbance, neurological disorders, solitary behaviour, rejection due to racial and socio-economic factors, aggressiveness, etc., often resulting to social maladjustment and marginalisation. Students follow the common core curriculum but they are provided with special teaching support in one or more subjects outside the school programme. A special class can be established with decision of the District Educational Authority, the school advisor of special education and the mainstream school unit of the student, according to the Presidential Decrees 603/82 and 472/83.

Teachers are expected to have deep knowledge of the learning difficulty, special training in selecting the appropriate pedagogical approach and accuracy in using the methodology needed in every case so as to motivate and help the student towards his/her inclusion in the mainstream class.

Cross-national category C

8. Socio-economic/cultural educational difficulties. This category has been included for the needs of this research, and classified in category C. Students of this category present social disadvantages, which rise from their socio-economic status as well as from their cultural and/or linguistic differentiations. Students of this category do not fall within the framework of the Law of Special Education. (Article 1. [3]: "Students whose mother tongue is not Greek, are not considered as students with special educational needs"). They are classified instead in the "Resource definition" as they are provided with extra help and special teaching support. Students of this category follow the common core curricula at primary and secondary level in the regular classes of the mainstream state system of education. Special programmes are planned and implemented by the Ministry of National Education with national and European Union funds.

Hungary

Cross-national category A

2. Moderate degree of mental disability. Moderate cognitive dysfunction based on organic central neural defect. It affects the intellectual functions, the learning abilities, the social adjustment and at a later stage independent living and working. Students frequently have other disabilities like physical, sensory and/or behavioural ones.

These students are typically in special schools or special classes attached to a special school for students with mild mental disability. The group does not follow the national curriculum only certain parts of it concentrating on the orientation in the close environment, on the development of communication skills and on certain elements of independence.

3. Visual disabilities. Visual impairment is officially regarded when the visual acuity in the corrected better eye is between 0 and 0.33 or the field of vision is not greater than 20 degrees because of an organic defect within the visual system. The category includes the following subcategories: blind students, students having low vision, partially sighted students and multi-handicapped visually impaired students. There exist two types of special schools for this group: the school for blind and the school for partially sighted, however the great majority of the latter group attends regular schools. Students belonging to this category follow the regular curriculum with a few modifications.

4. Hearing disabilities. Hearing impairment is considered when the hearing loss over the speech range (500-4000 Hz) effects the speech and language development and/or interferes with the ability to learn because of an organic defect within the auditory system. The category includes the following subcategories: deaf (average hearing loss approximately 90db or more), partially hearing (average hearing loss between approximately 40 and 89 dB) and hearing impaired multi-handicapped students.

There exist two types of special schools or classes for this group: the school for deaf and the school for partially hearing students. A growing number of partially hearing students attends regular schools. Students belonging to this category follow the regular curriculum with a few modifications.

5. Physical disability. Physical disability concerns the deficit of the posture and/or the restriction of mobility based on organic pathologies. The category includes several subcategories (cerebral motor disturbances, paraplegia, malformations, etc.) and students with or without multiple handicaps. There exist special schools for students with a physical disability. A growing number of these children attend the ordinary school system. Students belonging to this category follow the regular curriculum with a few modifications.

<u>Cross-national category B</u>

1. Mild degree of mental disability (learning disability). Mild cognitive dysfunction is a conclusion of the disturbed development of the learning ability. Students belonging to this category are permanent slow learners. The causes which hinder the development refer to abilities under the average and/or to the negative effects of the familiar, educational and socio-cultural environment. These children are mostly in special schools or in special classes attached to an ordinary school. Their placement into regular classes has recently started. Students belonging to this category follow a centrally modified national curriculum.

There exist certain regulations – like individual developmental plans, alternative evaluation in the primary, prolongation of primary one – to prevent students from getting into this category.

6. Speech disorders. Mostly temporary problems of speech development and/or speech intelligibility (about 96% dyslalia, about 2% delayed speech development and about 2% stuttering). Almost all students attend regular schools and receive speech therapy in their free time except those who attend one of the two special schools for children with severe disorders.

7. Other disabilities. Different forms of learning disorders (reading, spelling, writing, mathematical abilities) on the basis of partial cognitive dysfunctions. Further on, students with attention deficits, emotional problems, hyperactivity, severe behaviour problems, autism.

Most of these students attend the regular school system, although some in remedial classes attached to the regular schools. There are only a few special classes for this category. Students follow the regular curriculum with certain modifications if necessary.

<u>Cross-national category C</u>

8. Disadvantaged pupils. Students living in families, where the conditions – as a consequence of parents' behaviour and/or poor social situation – hinder the child's normal physical, intellectual, emotional or moral development, but the child is not considered as disabled. Families with low income might get additional financial help to support the student's education. The disadvantaged pupils are officially registered in the schools. The category falls outside of the Hungarian definition of disability (special educational needs).

Italy

<u>Cross-national category A</u>

1. Visual impairment. Includes blind children and partially sighted children.

2. Hearing impairment. Includes deaf children and partially deaf children.

3. Moderate mental handicap. This category includes both mild mental retardation and moderate mental retardation. It includes therefore those pupils who are classified as "educable" (that is, who can acquire the knowledge in skills demanded of the final year of primary education – age 10-11) and as "trainable" (that is, who can acquire the knowledge in skills demanded of the second year of primary education – age 7-8). The IQ levels of these pupils range from 70 to 35-40.

4. Severe mental handicap. This category includes both the group with serious mental retardation and the group with most serious mental retardation. It includes pupils who can at most acquire a minimum level of communicative language and pupils who at most can acquire very basic self-care and communication skills. The IQ levels of these pupils range from 35-40 to under 20-25.

5. Mild physical handicap. Children with slight physical impairments that should not prevent them from becoming relatively autonomous.

6. Severe physical handicap. Children with severe physical impairments profoundly affecting personal autonomy. These children require adequate and continuous assistance.

7. Multiple handicap. Children with two or more of the impairments included in categories 1 to 6. Residual category.

Cross-national category C
8. Students with foreign citizenship. Pupils with a foreign citizenship do not directly receive additional resources but benefit rather from the resources allocated to schools to promote and increase activities/projects of inclusion, *e.g.* intercultural education, language training, etc.

Japan

Cross-national category A
1. Blind and partially sighted. Those with corrected visual acuity of less than 0.1 for both eyes. Those with corrected visual acuity of over 0.1 but less than 0.3 and who require education through Braille or who will require such education in the future. Impairment of visual functions other than visual acuity such as contraction of visual field and who require education through Braille or who will require such as education in the future.
2. Deaf and hard of hearing. Those with a hearing level of more than 100 decibels for both ears. Those with a hearing level of more than 60 decibels but less than 100 decibels and who find it either impossible or extremely difficult to comprehend normal speech even with a hearing aid.
3. Intellectual disabilities. Severe – moderate – mild and those who particularly lack social adaptability.
4. Physically disabled. Those who find it impossible or extremely difficult to maintain their posture, write, or walk, and those with similar disabilities. Those with milder disabilities and who require medical observation and guidance for more than six months.
5. Health impaired. Those with a chronic disease of heart, chest or kidney and who require more than six months of medical care or restricted living. Those who are physically weak and require more than six months of restricted living.
6. Speech impaired. Those with speech impairment other than with speech impairment resulting from deafness, hard of hearing, cerebral palsy, and intellectual disabilities.
7. Emotionally disturbed. Those with emotional disturbance but excluding those with emotional disturbance accompanied by intellectual disability or health impairment.

Cross-national category C
8. Students who require Japanese instruction

Korea

Cross-national category A
1. Visual impairments
1) A person with a visual acuity of below 0.04 in both eyes after the correction.
2) A person has possibility of being educated not by vision but only by Braille or listening because of severe visual impairments.
3) A person with a corrective visual acuity of over 0.04 but who cannot perform visual tasks with specific learning materials or modification of tasks.
4) A person who can perform visual tasks only with specific materials and equipments.
2. Hearing impairments
1) A person with a hearing loss of 90 dB or over in both ears.
2) A person who is incapable of or severely deficient in language comprehension with a hearing aid due to severe hearing loss.
3) A person who has partial hearing affecting language use, and thereby having difficulty in normal schooling.

3. Mental retardation. A person with IQ below 75 with deficiency in adaptive behaviours.

4. Physical impairments. A person who has disability in physical functioning and has difficulty in supporting limb movement, and thereby has difficulty in normal schooling.

6. Speech impairments. A person who has problems in articulation, fluency, voice, and verbalisation, and thereby has difficulty in communication and learning.

8. Otherwise physical and psychological impairments

Cross-national category B

5. Emotional disturbance

1) A person with an inability to learn that cannot be explained by intellectual, sensory and health factors.

2) A person who has an inability to build or maintain satisfactory interpersonal relationships with peers and teachers.

3) Inappropriate types of behaviors or feelings under normal circumstances.

4) A general pervasive mood of unhappiness or depression.

5) A tendency to develop physical symptoms or fears associated with personal or school problems.

6) A person who has difficulty in response toward sensory stimulus, language, cognitive ability or interpersonal relationship.

7. Learning disabilities. A person who has specific learning problems such as maths, speaking, reading or writing.

Mexico*

Cross-national category A

1. Blindness. Children or youth without visual faculty or whose visual faculty is largely impaired. Optical correction does not improve their visual capacity and they cannot function like seeing persons. This is usually a permanent condition. Blind persons require alternative options and/or equipment for curriculum accessibility. They have serious problems of displacement and need special instruction to obtain autonomy for self-care. Blindness does not affect intellectual performance.

2. Partial visual disability. It is the diminution of the visual sharpness in both eyes. People with partial visual disability benefit from optical supports such as: magnifying glasses, eyeglasses, binoculars or amplifying screens, but they cannot read regular size text or images. They can overcome problems for curriculum accessibility through special equipment or alternative written language supports. They need references to be able to move from one place to another. Regularly they can only see shades or bulks. Visual disability can be progressive until it becomes blindness. This condition does not affect the person's intellectual performance.

3. Intellectual disability. This category includes different grades of intellectual disability which, in Mexico, used to be related to IQ. Since legislation for the adoption of the integration policy, intellectual disability was re-conceptualised. Now it is categorised in relation to the child's performance in his/her interaction with the environment. It implies significant sub-average general intellectual functioning, learning difficulties and slow development of adaptive behaviour, all of which affect a child's educational performance. In the school context, students with intellectual disability show more difficulties than the rest of his or her peers to understand instructions, abstract concepts and metaphorical or figurative language. As a result, they show dependent conduct and require support to finish any learning activity, especially when it involves a new concept or concept relations. They demand more interactivity with the environment to understand concepts and to have longer periods of attention and concentration.

In synthesis, they require full interaction with an enriched learning context for the development of basic learning competence and skills. Children with intellectual disability are also slow in the development of social skills and in the control of their emotional feelings and reactions. Most of these minors can attend basic education in the regular school, with support and curricular adaptations, including flexibility.

4. Auditory or hearing disability. The auditory disability is a superficial to moderate loss of hearing. Persons with auditory disability can benefit from the use of a hearing aid to perceive oral language and develop it. Children with auditory disability can develop a great ability for lip-reading as a strategy for better oral language comprehension and thus, better communication skills. This condition does not affect the person's intellectual performance. Some children with mild hearing disability can also learn sign language as a first or second language to communicate with non-oral deaf persons or to act as interpreters.

5. Deafness or severe auditory disability. Deafness is a severe sensorial impairment that does not allow hearing and (therefore) the development of oral language. Deaf children use sign language as their mother tongue but can also learn the national oral language after special education intervention. They must learn written language as means of communication with the hearing population and for accessibility to the written learning environment (books, letters, notes, computer information, etc.). They can also develop lip-reading skills to facilitate and enhance their communication with the majority hearing society. Deafness does not affect the person's intellectual performance, but the development of a sign, oral or written language is necessary for the complete development of their intellectual potential and their accessibility to the basic learning curricular competencies.

6. Motor disability. This category includes moderate to severe motor disability.

Moderate motor disability: when the person's motor condition is determined by peripheral damage. This means that the disability is partial and only affects the movement or the co-ordination of movements of specific parts of the body.

Severe motor disability: when the person's motor condition is determined by central neurological damage that affects the overall movements (as in cerebral palsy).

In both cases but in different degrees, architectonic, physical adaptations of the school environment are required to enhance accessibility, as well as the use of special school furniture and equipment in classrooms. The provision of these adaptations determines success in the integration of children with motor disability to mainstream education. Students with severe motor disability require additional adaptations and supports for fine co-ordination of movements for speech pronunciation, writing, drawing and other skills related to inputs and outputs of the learning context. Motor disability is generally a permanent condition but does not affect the person's intellectual potential.

7. Multiple disability. Students with two or more of the disabilities included in categories 1 to 6.

Cross-national category B

8. Learning difficulties. Children evidence their difficulties when starting primary school or as soon as they start formal contact with the school curriculum, especially in reading, writing or mathematics. They do not have disabilities and they evidence average or above average intelligence. Normally, their language development is good, although, some of them have associated speech pronunciation problems. These difficulties are not associated with disadvantages, and have been recently classified as a disruption between the child and the learning context. Learning difficulties are often transitory and can be overcome with transformation of the learning environment, especially through teachers' orientation to significant learning in the classroom in contrast with mechanical, non-significant learning.

Cross-national category C

10. Compensatory educational needs. Compensatory education needs are those present in all students who attend regular, general or indigenous education services, which have limitations in structure, equipment, stability of the teaching staff and/or low productivity in the school performance indicators. Therefore, additional resources are supplied to the school and/or to the children to assure their access to the school curriculum and the acquisition of basic learning competence with quality and equity. This category also includes students from poor zones of the country who receive economic scholarship from the OPORTUNIDADES programme, intended to support their enrolment, regular attendance and completion of school.

11. Communitary educational needs. Students that live in small communities of less than 500 inhabitants, with high marginality, extreme poverty and population dispersion. These communities lack regular basic schooling services and, in general, have linguistic and cultural characteristics of their own, different from those that define behavioural patterns of the national school culture.

12. Indigenous communitary educational needs. Indigenous education promotes the development of capabilities and skills of those who belong to cultural and linguistic contexts of indigenous Mexican groups. The educational models are suited to the specific conditions and characteristics of the different cultural and ethnic groups. Largely due to the isolation and population dispersion of the majority of their settlements throughout the national territory, these indigenous people suffer from severe underdevelopment, which reduces their living standards and limits their possibilities for growth. The general aims and objectives of the national curriculum encompass the education provided to indigenous children and grant the necessary adaptations to cater to Mexico's cultural diversity.

13. Migrant educational needs. The migrant agricultural population goes from its hometown to another economic region or zone where temporal workforce is required. 60% belongs to diverse ethnic groups with a majority of monolingual or incipiently bilingual members. They live during the harvest period in agricultural camps, which they share with migrants from other ethnic groups. The many migratory routes, the diversity of cultures and languages that converge in each camp, and the difficulty to foresee the length of the agricultural cycles have a negative impact in planning and delivery of the educational services targeted to these workers and their families.

* Category 9. Outstanding capabilities and skills. These children are described as those who show above average skills in one or several areas of knowledge. Access to curriculum looks easy for them; they show commitment with learning, they are persistent in the fulfilment of tasks and show great creativity in problem solving. Frequently, they show special talents in one or more academic, personal or social areas.

Netherlands

Cross-national category A

1. Deaf children. A pupil is admissible to special education if he/she has a loss of hearing > 80dB (without hearing aid) or the pupil has a loss of hearing between 70-80 dB and is completely "deaf-functioning".

2. Hard of hearing. A pupil is admissible to special education if he/she has a loss of hearing between 35dB and 80 dB (without hearing aid). Pupils with a hearing-loss between 70dB and 80dB who are not considered to be "deaf-functioning" (see 1). Besides this it should be made clear that the pupil due to his/her handicap has a structural problem in attending (mainstream) education. This is the case if a pupil has severe problems in the development of speech and language or due to the handicap, severe learning difficulties or social-emotional problems.

3. Language and communication disabilities. A pupil is admissible to special education if a speech/language disorder has been proven (if possible in connection with a communication problem) on one or more of the following terrains: speech production, speech perception and/or defects in the syntactical, lexical and semantical knowledge. Learning difficulties are due to the speech/language disorder.

4. Visual handicap. This category includes blind and partially sighted. A pupil is admissible when the visual acuity is <0.3 or the field of vision is not greater than 30 degrees. This category also includes pupils with a visual handicap in combination with a mental handicap (multi-handicapped pupils).

5. Physically handicapped/motor impairment. This category includes pupils with congenital and non-congenital disorders or dysfunctions. The pupils in this type of education have serious neurological or orthopedic problems and are in need of regular medical or paramedical treatment or assistance and/or special teaching materials. It has to be proven that the pupil cannot attend mainstream education with technical aids and support from or within a special school is needed.

6. Other health impairments. This category includes pupils with chronic illnesses, like heart diseases, respiratory disorders, diabetes, epilepsy and such who need regular (para-)medical assistance and treatment. This category also includes pupils with neurological or psychiatric problems. Pupils with motor impairments are not included in this category. The illness/disorder has to affect the educational performance of the pupil in such a way that special education is indicated.

8. Mental handicaps (severe learning disabilities). This category includes pupils with a profound, severe, moderate and mild mental handicap. IQ: < 60 or between 60 and 70 with a low social self-reliance level.

9. Behaviour disabilities. This category includes pupils with severe behaviour problems. Most of them have psychiatric, neurological or developmental disorders like Autism (PDD-NOS and Asperger included), ODD, Tourettes syndrome, severe ADHD, they suffer from serious depression or psychosis (DSM-IV classified). Often a combination of disorders or a combination of a disorder with a low average IQ leads to the transfer to special education. Due to the disorder these pupils have severe social-emotional problems not only at school but also at home and during recreation and leisure activities. Due to the disorder the development and the learning process of these pupils is seriously disturbed: pupils don't benefit enough from education. Extra support in mainstream education has been proven unsuccessful. Admittance to special education gives them a chance to benefit more from education, since special schools for behaviour disorders have more possibilities to support pupils in their learning process.

10. Chronic conditions requiring paediological institutes. Admittance to this type of special education is possible if there is a serious behaviour problem and due to that a serious disturbance of the development of the pupil. At the moment of admittance the nature of the disorder is not clear. During this period the pupil is placed in this type of school, the pupil is observed, diagnosed and treated. After a limited period the pupil is transferred to another special school or transferred with support to a mainstream school. A limited number of pupils will stay in these schools till transfer to secondary education.

11. Multiply handicapped. A pupil is admissible to this type of special education if he/she has a combination of a mental handicap and a physical or sensory handicap.

<u>Cross-national category B</u>
7. Learning and behaviour difficulties. This category includes pupils with heterogeneous (learning and behaviour) difficulties like ADHD, PDD-NOS, dyslexia or pupils with a low average IQ. It concerns pupils for whom support within mainstream primary education has been not enough. Their problems are not severe enough for referral to special education. They are referred to a school for special primary education. These schools (or special classes) work with the same curriculum as the mainstream schools, but the classes are smaller and there is more specialised support available.

13. Children in vocational training with learning difficulties. Pupils can be admitted to special classes within the mainstream system for secondary education if they have learning difficulties due to their cognitive possibilities (IQ: > 60 < 80) and as a result of that will not be able to finish mainstream secondary education with a certificate. These pupils are prepared for transition to the labour market. Another group is the group pupils with an IQ between 75-90, learning difficulties and serious social emotional problems and a group with a higher IQ but with severe social emotional problems due to, for example, autism. Education is aimed at gaining a diploma/certificate.

<u>Cross-national category C</u>
12. Children from disadvantaged backgrounds. Schools receive additional funding for pupils, who have a social-ethnic or social economic disadvantaged background.

Poland

Cross-national category A

1. Light mental handicap. Light mental handicap covers handicaps as connecting with intelligence, cognitive processes, memory and thinking. Persons with light mental handicap (IQ between 51 and 67) are capable of learning practical skills, reading, writing and notions of arithmetic thanks to special education (and who can be taught a certain degree of socialisation).

2. Moderate and severe mental handicap. Moderate handicap (IQ between 36 and 51) – pupils able to acquire simple notions of communication, simple manual skills, hygiene and elementary safety, but they are incapable of learning arithmetic or reading.

Severe mental handicap (IQ between 20 and 35) – pupils with severe mental handicap benefit from the systematic learning of simple gestures.

3. Profound mental handicap. Profound mental handicap (IQ between 0 and 19) – pupils with profound mental handicap have severe problems with learning simple gestures.

4. Blind. Total lack of sight. Acuity of sight on level 0-1/20 healthy acuity of sight, or acuity of sight no larger than 1/20 healthy acuity of sight, limited field of vision no longer than 20 degrees, regardless of acuity of sight. Blind pupils cannot read at the close distance printing Sn.1.5 even after correction.

5. Partially sighted. Acuity of sight between 1/20 and 5/20 healthy acuity of sight; field of vision limited to 30 degrees, regardless of acuity of sight (acuity of sight can be better than 5/20 healthy acuity of sight). Partially sighted pupils can read better with seeing eye after correction printing Sn. 1.5 at close distance.

6. Deaf. Lack perception of sounds or loss of hearing above 90 dB.

7. Partially hearing. Loss of hearing between 40 and 89 dB; students have to use a hearing aid.

8. Chronically sick. Refers to students who suffer from various psychosomatic illnesses. It is the reason of long-lasting hospital, health resort or home treatment. Schooling are organised in hospitals, health resorts. Organisation and range of classes are adjusted to abilities of sick children.

9. Motion handicap. Refers to students with various forms of motor dysfunction based on impairment of organs of movement. Students have to use: artificial limb, wheelchair or others.

13. Autistic. Refers to students with non-specific developmental disturbance since birth. Autistic students present psychomotor problems, which prevent them from being included in the social environment and the regular educational system. Developmental disability significantly affecting verbal and non-verbal communication and social interaction. Other characteristics often associated with autism are engagement in repetitive activities and stereotyped movements, resistance to environmental change or change in daily routines.

14. Multiple handicap. Refers to students with at least two coexistent impairments of sensorial, mental or motion origin.

Cross-national category B

11. Behaviour difficulties. Refers to students, whose behaviour makes their social functioning difficult. Symptoms of behaviour difficulties include: stoppage, retiring (withdraw) or opposite – psychomotoric expansion, over-excitability (hyperactive).

12. Danger to addiction. Refers to students whose behaviour runs the risk for physical, psychical health or social relationship.

15. Remedial classes. Remedial classes are organised for pupils with substantial lack of education and skills, to help them intensively achieve level of education and skills adequate to educational core at their educational stage.

16. Therapeutic classes. Therapeutic classes are organised for pupils with homogenous or multiple disorders requiring adaptation of teaching organisation and process to their special needs education and long-lasting special help.

17. Remedial occupations. Remedial occupations are organised for pupils with severe retardation in education at their educational stage. Number of pupils taking part in remedial occupations should be 4-8 persons.

18. Compensatory occupations. Compensatory occupations are organised for pupils with specific learning difficulties making impossible achievements of education and skills adequate to educational core at their educational stage. Number of pupils taking part in compensatory occupations should be 2-5 persons.

19. Individual education. Pupils whose health condition makes impossible or difficult taking part in regular school or pre-school education. Student/pupil individually educated stays student/pupil of school or kindergarten, which organised for him/her this education.

Cross-national category C

10. Social disadvantages. Refers to students who do not accept current social norms. It manifests itself as anti-social behaviour, inability to function in the group, disturbance of emotional process. Students with social disadvantage can be injurious for individuals and for social environment; it appears in criminal, neurotic and psychopathic acts.

Slovak Republic

Cross-national category A

1. Hearing impairment. Loss of hearing of different degree, type and origin of disease. Classification from the point of view of education: moderate loss of hearing (up to 70dB); severe loss of hearing (70 dB and more). Education derives from the degree of loss of hearing and age, at which the impairment appeared. Specific methods for creation and development of language, special educational aids and in some cases special educational programmes are used in the process of education.

2. Visual impairment. This category includes a) blind, b) partially sighted, c) dim-sighted, d) squint-eyed – this means with disorders of binocular eyesight. In the instructional process the educational programmes for regular schools with inclusion of some specific subjects, special educational methods and special compensation aids are applied. In education of blind pupils the textbooks and other teaching texts in Braille are required.

3. Physical disability. Inborn or gained defects of movement and supporting system, or impairment of the nerve system, if demonstrated by impaired motion. In the instructional process the educational programmes for regular schools with inclusion of some specific subjects, special educational aids and methods are applied.

4. Speech disorders. Impaired ability of verbal form of interpersonal communication, which can be demonstrated as speechless – developmental, organ or neurotic, sound disturbance, disturbance of articulation and continuity of speech. In instructional process either educational programmes for regular schools, including specific subjects for development of communication skills or specific educational programmes for speechless pupils are applied. Special instructional methods and the assistance of speech therapist are required.

5. Moderate mental retardation. Intellectual disability of the IQ level between 51-70. Pupils receive basic education and vocational training. In the process of education the special curriculum adaptation and specific instructional methods are required. After education they are basically capable of integration into regular social and professional environments.

6. Middle-severe mental retardation. Intellectual disability of the IQ level less than 50. In the process of education specific educational programmes or in individual cases individual educational plans are applied to receive basic social and vocational skills. After education some of them are able to work in the sheltered environment (workshops).

7. Autism. A psychotic condition leading to the isolation of an individual in his internal world, own pictures, reduced level of social contact even to the level of isolation, lack of emotional contact with environment. The specific educational programmes and the specific methods are used in education.

11. Multiple impairment. A combination of several handicaps, which results not in a simple addition, but in a new individual variable quality. Most frequently, it is a combination of mental handicap with hearing, sight, body handicap, speech and behaviour disorders or social maladjustment. In special vocational school they are prepared for simple manual activities. Special educational methods are applied.

12. Sick and physically weak children in medical facilities. Those who in the given time are hospitalised in a hospital or medical facilities, sanatoriums and convalescent homes. These are children with long-term (chronic) diseases, after injuries, operations, with weakened health. Depending on relevant health condition, children can learn in accordance with specific educational programmes for special kindergarten or primary schools or educational programmes for regular schools.

Cross-national category B

8. Learning difficulties. Impaired communication ability from the point of view of graphic side of speech (dyslexia and dyscalculia). In instructional process the educational programmes (including specific subject for development of the communication skills) for regular schools and specific instructional methods are applied.

9. Behavioural disorders. Non-adaptive forms of individual behaviour, which are unfavourably demonstrated in social relations and in the socialisation process of individual. It is a broad spectrum of maladaptive forms of behaviour, which are causing educational problems and are based on biologic–psychological equipment of an individual (weakened body, diseases, organic damage of CNS, uneven development of processes of maturing of personality, ADD and ADHD syndromes) and on the other hand, socially unsuitable educational influence and cultural background (family, school), or it is a combination of both factors. The co-operation of teachers and psychologist or special teacher in education is required.

Cross-national category C

10. Social maladjustment. Non-adaptive forms of behaviour, breaching ethical, legal and other social standards, and the individual did not reach the age of criminal responsibility or legal standards for juveniles are valid. Children and juveniles with such degree of impaired psycho-social development will be placed in special educational establishments with the purpose of a re-education (10-18 years of age).

Spain*

Cross-national category A

1. Hearing impaired. Students with partial or complete hearing loss.

2. Motor impaired. Motor system alteration due to a deficient osteoarticularm muscular and/or nervous system activity.

3. Visual impaired. Significant or complete vision loss.

4. Mental handicap. Intellectual performance significantly below average and substantial limitations in adoptive development, revealed before age 18.

5. Serious personality disorders, psychosis and autism. Personality alteration, generally linked with psychosis and autism.

6. Multiple impairment. Two or more concurrent disabilities.

9. Students in hospitals or with health problems. For students who have serious health problems and are hospitalised or housebound.

Cross-national category B

11. Learning difficulties. Refers to temporary learning difficulties (dyslexia is included in this category).

12. Curricular diversification. For students who encounter difficulties at the second stage of the compulsory secondary education. It consists specifically of a programme that must ensure individualised teaching. The curricular content is adapted and a specific methodology is employed to allow them to complete successfully the above mentioned stage.

Cross-national category C
8. Students with compensatory educational needs. For students with social or cultural problems which are the cause of a delay in the achievement of knowledge.
10. Children of itinerant workers. For students whose parents are itinerant workers (temporary, circus, fair).

* Category 7. Highly gifted. Intellectual capability above average, high degree of devotion to task and creativity level.

Sweden

Cross-national category A
1. Pupils with impaired hearing, vision and physical disabilities. Special schools exist for deaf, hard-of-hearing, sight-impaired and speech- or language-impaired children with secondary disabilities. There are eight special schools in Sweden with approximately 800 students. Most intellectually handicapped children, though, attend compulsory school for those with learning difficulties (cat. 2) or are integrated in regular schools (cat. 5, 6). Special school is of ten years' duration and has its own syllabuses. Term grades are awarded from year 9 and leaving certificates are awarded at the end of year 10. The same rules apply to the assessment of grades as in compulsory school, but the criteria are in respect of year 10 (instead of 9). Suitable parts of those national tests used in compulsory school may be used in special school.
2. Students with mental retardation. Compulsory school and upper secondary school for mentally retarded students has the same curriculum as other compulsory and upper secondary schools but has its own syllabuses, adapted to this type of schooling and the pupils. Compulsory school for mentally retarded comprises compulsory basic school for the mentally handicapped and training school. It involves nine years of compulsory schooling and in addition to this, pupils are entitled to a tenth, optional school year to supplement their education. Compulsory basic schools for the mentally handicapped are attended by pupils with minor difficulties. They are basically taught the same subjects as pupils in regular compulsory schools. However, the content and scope of the subjects are adapted according to aptitude, with an individual teaching plan for each pupil. Training school pupils have disabilities which prevent them from assimilating instruction in compulsory school for mentally handicapped. Instead of individual subjects, the training school syllabus has five teaching areas, which together are intended to foster sound all round development.
Upper secondary school for those with learning difficulties offers vocational education in the same way as regular upper secondary in the form of national, specially designed or individual programmes. All programmes last four years, apart from individual programmes, and include core subjects and programme-specific subjects. Pupils attending compulsory and upper secondary school for mentally retarded students must be issued with a certificate on completion of their studies. A final assessment is also obtainable on request.
3. Students with impaired hearing and physical disabilities. Defined as students in need of special support in their schooling because of their disabilities. Students with impaired hearing and physical disabilities from all over the country can apply to five regular upper secondary schools in Sweden.

Cross-national category C
4. Students receiving tuition in mother tongue (other than Swedish) and/or Swedish as a second language. According to the Education Act and national guidelines all students are entitled to tuition in their mother tongue and tuition in Swedish as a second language if, for example, one or both parents has/have another mother tongue than Swedish and this language is frequently used at home (for more detailed information on students rights, etc., see the Education Act).

Switzerland

The classifications and the assignment of various special schools and classes to categories of special educational needs were established by the *Schweizerische Zentralstelle für Heilpädagogik* (Swiss Secretariat for Special Education) in co-operation with the cantonal experts. An exact national definition of categories is not available.

Cross-national category A

9. Students with a mental handicap – educable mental handicap: special schools

The Swiss Federal Disability Insurance has laid down the following eligibility criteria to receive additional resources for schooling: insured persons with mental retardation, with IQs of 75 and below.

10. Students with a mental handicap – trainable mental handicap: special schools

The Swiss Federal Disability Insurance has laid down the following eligibility criteria to receive additional resources for schooling: insured persons with mental retardation, with IQs of 75 and below.

11. Students with a mental handicap – multiply handicapped: special schools

The Swiss Federal Disability Insurance has laid down the following eligibility criteria to receive additional resources for schooling: insured persons with mental retardation, with IQs of 75 and below.

12. Physical disabilities: special schools

The Swiss Federal Disability Insurance has laid down the following eligibility criteria to receive additional resources for schooling: insured persons with a severe physical disability.

13. Behaviour disorders: special schools

The Swiss Federal Disability Insurance has laid down the following eligibility criteria to receive additional resources for schooling: insured persons with a severe behavioural disturbance.

14. Deaf or hard of hearing: special schools

The Swiss Federal Disability Insurance has laid down the following eligibility criteria to receive additional resources for schooling: insured persons with hearing impairment or deafness, with a medium hearing loss of the better ear of at least 30 dB or an equivalent hearing loss on a language audiogram.

15. Language disability: special schools

The Swiss Federal Disability Insurance has laid down the following eligibility criteria to receive additional resources for schooling: insured persons with a severe language impairment

16. Visual handicap: special schools

The Swiss Federal Disability Insurance has laid down the following eligibility criteria to receive additional resources for schooling: insured persons with visual impairment or blindness, with a corrected vision which is less than 0.3 in both eyes.

17. Chronic conditions/prolonged hospitalisation: special schools

18. Multiple disabilities: special schools

The Swiss Federal Disability Insurance has laid down the following eligibility criteria to receive additional resources for schooling: insured persons for whom none of the particular single criteria applies but who are multiply affected due to a combination of the above leading to a health impairment and therefore to an inability to participate in the regular school system.

Cross-national category B

1. Learning disabilities – introductory classes: special classes

2. Learning disabilities – special classes: special classes

3. Learning disabilities – vocationally oriented classes: special classes

4. Behavioural difficulties: special classes

6. Physical disabilities: special classes

7. Sensory and language impairments: special classes

8. Students who are ill/hospital classes: special classes

19. Others of the group "special curriculum": special classes

Cross-national category C

5. Foreign first language: special classes

Turkey*

Cross-national category A

1. Visual impairment. A condition characterised by a partial or total absence of vision that negatively affects the educational performance and social adjustment of the individual.

2. Hearing impairment. A condition characterised by a difficulty in learning of the speech, use of language and communication due to a partial or total absence of hearing sensitivity that negatively affects the educational performance and social adjustment of the individual.

3. Orthopedic impairment. A condition characterised by a disease, defect and disability in the skeleton, muscles and joints that negatively affect the educational performance and social adjustment of the individual.

4. Moderate learning disability. A condition characterised by a delayed language and speech development, the manifestation of social, emotional, or behavioural problems as well as a delayed acquisition of reading-writing and arithmetic skills.

5. Severe learning disability. A condition characterised by a significantly delayed language and speech development, a manifestation of significant social, emotional or behavioural problems as well as a delayed acquisition of basic self-help skills.

6. Language and speech difficulty. A difficulty in the use of language, learning of speech, and communication due to an impairment and disorder occurred in verbal communication in different levels and forms that negatively affect the educational performance and social adjustment of the individual.

8. Chronic illness. Having an illness which occurred during the developmental period, requiring permanent care and treatment that negatively affect the educational performance and social adjustment of the individual.

9. Neurological injury. A neurological defect which occurred during the developmental period that negatively affects the educational performance and social adjustment of the individual.

13. Autism. A condition that is evident in early childhood period, significantly and negatively affecting verbal and non-verbal communication, educational performance and social adjustment of the individual.

Cross-national category B

10. Specific learning difficulty. A condition in one or more of the information processing areas involved in understanding or in using language, characterised by an inadequate capacity to listen, speak, read, write, spell, concentrate, or in arithmetic operations that negatively affects the educational performance and social adjustment of the individual.

11. Emotional adjustment difficulty. A condition that lasts over a long period of time and cannot be explained by health, mental, or emotional factors; exhibited by one or more of the characteristics such as an inability to build and maintain satisfactory intra and interpersonal relationships; a general mood of unhappiness and depression or the physical symptoms such as the fears, biting ones nails, sucking the fingers due to personal or school problems that negatively affect educational performance and social adjustment of the individual.

Cross-national category C

12. Social adjustment difficulty. A condition that is characterised by risky living conditions, drug abuse, malnutrition, immigration, delinquency, work, neglect, abuse, abandonment, and language differences that negatively affect the educational performance and social adjustment of the individual.

* 7. Gifted or talented. Having exceptional abilities in academic areas and/or arts that result in higher levels of performance compared to their peers.

United Kingdom – England

<u>Cross-national category A</u>
1. Children with statements (records) of special educational needs. The statement (record) of special educational needs is a legal document that sets out the child's needs and all the special help he or she should have, which may include money, staff time and special equipment. It also sets out the responsibility for these resources between the school, local authority and others agencies such as health and social services. The statement (record) will also specify the educational placement of the child – whether in mainstream (regular) school, special school or other form of specialist provision. In England, Wales and Northern Ireland, the vast majority of pupils in special schools will have a statement. In Scotland, a smaller proportion of pupils in special schools will have records.

<u>Cross-national category B</u>
2. Children with special educational needs without statements (records)

United States

<u>Cross-national category A</u>
1. Mental retardation. "Mental retardation" means significantly sub-average general intellectual functioning existing concurrently with deficits in adaptive behaviour and manifested during the developmental period that adversely affects a child's educational performance (34 Code of Federal Regulations §300.7).
2. Speech or language impairment. "Speech or language impairment" means a communication disorder such as stuttering, impaired articulation, a language impairment, or a voice impairment that adversely affects a child's educational performance (34 Code of Federal Regulations §300.7).
3. Visual impairments. "Visual impairment including blindness" means an impairment in vision that, even with correction, adversely affects a child's educational performance. The term includes both partial sight and blindness (34 Code of Federal Regulations §300.7).
5. Orthopedic impairments. "Orthopedic impairment" means a severe orthopedic impairment that adversely affects a child's educational performance. The term includes impairments caused by congenital anomaly (*e.g.* clubfoot, absence of some member, etc.), impairments caused by disease (*e.g.* poliomyelitis, bone tuberculosis, etc.), and impairments from other causes (*e.g.* cerebral palsy, amputations, and fractures or burns that cause contractures) (34 Code of Federal Regulations §300.7).
6. Other health impairments. "Other health impairment" means having limited strength, vitality or alertness, due to chronic or acute health problems such as a heart condition, tuberculosis, rheumatic fever, nephritis, asthma, sickle cell anaemia, haemophilia, epilepsy, lead poisoning, leukaemia, or diabetes that adversely affect a child's educational performance (34 Code of Federal Regulations §300.7).
8. Deaf/blindness. "Deaf/blindness" means concomitant hearing and visual impairments, the combination of which causes such severe communication and other developmental and educational problems that they cannot be accommodated in special education programmes solely for children with deafness or children with blindness (34 Code of Federal Regulations §300.7).
9. Multiple disabilities. "Multiple disabilities" means concomitant impairments (such as mental retardation-blindness, mental retardation-orthopedic impairment, etc.), the combination of which causes such severe educational problems that they cannot be accommodated in special education programmes solely for one of the impairments. The term does not include deaf/blindness (34 Code of Federal Regulations §300.7).
10. Hearing impairments. Hearing impairment includes deafness and hard of hearing. "Deafness" means a hearing impairment that is so severe that the child is impaired in processing linguistic information through hearing, with or without amplification, that adversely affects a child's educational performance. "Hard of hearing" means an impairment in hearing, whether permanent or fluctuating, that adversely affects a child's educational performance but that is not included under the definition of deafness in this section (34 Code of Federal Regulations §300.7).

11. Autism. "Autism" means a developmental disability significantly affecting verbal and non-verbal communication and social interaction, generally evident before age 3, that adversely affects a child's educational performance. Other characteristics often associated with autism are engagement in repetitive activities and stereotyped movements, resistance to environmental change or change in daily routines, and unusual responses to sensory experiences. The term does not apply if a child's educational performance is adversely affected primarily because the child has a serious emotional disturbance (34 Code of Federal Regulations §300.7).

12. Traumatic brain injury. "Traumatic brain injury" means an acquired injury to the brain caused by an external physical force, resulting in total or partial functional disability or psychosocial impairment, or both, that adversely affects a child's educational performance. The term applies to open or closed head injuries resulting in impairments in one or more areas, such as cognition; language; memory; attention; reasoning; abstract thinking; judgement; problem-solving; sensory; perceptual and motor abilities; psychosocial behaviour; physical functions; information processing; and speech. The term does not apply to brain injuries that are congenital or degenerative, or brain injuries induced by birth trauma (34 Code of Federal Regulations §300.7).

13. Developmental delay. "Developmental delay" means a student "who is experiencing developmental delays, as defined by the State and as measured by appropriate diagnostic instruments and procedures, in one or more of the following areas: physical development, cognitive development, communication development, social or emotional development, or adaptive development and who, by reason thereof, needs special education and related services" (34 Code of Federal Regulations §300.7[b][1][2], 300.313[b]).

Cross-national category B

4. Emotional disturbance. "Emotional disturbance" is defined as follows: (i) The term means a condition exhibiting one or more of the following characteristics over a long period of time and to a marked degree that adversely affects a child's educational performance – (A) An inability to learn that cannot be explained by intellectual, sensory, or health factors; (B) An inability to build or maintain satisfactory interpersonal relationships with peers and teachers; (C) Inappropriate types of behaviour or feelings under normal circumstances; (D) A general pervasive mood of unhappiness or depression; or (E) A tendency to develop physical symptoms or fears associated with personal or school problems. (ii) The term includes schizophrenia. The term does not apply to children who are socially maladjusted, unless it is determined that they have a serious emotional disturbance (34 Code of Federal Regulations §300.7).

7. Specific learning disability. "Specific learning disability" means a disorder in one or more of the basic psychological processes involved in understanding or in using language, spoken or written, that may manifest itself in an imperfect ability to listen, think, speak, read, write, spell, or to do mathematical calculations. The term includes such conditions as perceptual disabilities, brain injury, minimal brain dysfunction, dyslexia, and developmental aphasia. The term does not apply to children who have learning problems that are primarily the result of visual, hearing, or motor disabilities, of mental retardation, of emotional disturbance, or of environmental, cultural, or economic disadvantage (34 Code of Federal Regulations §300.7).

Cross-national category C
14. Title 1 – Disadvantaged students

Chapter 3
Analysis of the quantitative data based on categories used nationally

Background

This chapter analyses the data provided by countries in Tables 2, 3 and 4 of the electronic questionnaire (covering special schools, special classes and regular classes respectively) by national categories of disability, learning difficulties and disadvantages based on the resources definition given in Chapter 1. This analysis follows an identical format to that in the corresponding chapter in the earlier publication *Equity in Education: Students with Disabilities, Learning Difficulties and Disadvantages* (OECD, 2004) which was based on the 1998/99 round of data collection.

Individual country data will be available on the CERI website, *www.oecd.org/edu/equity/senddd* in due course. The data cover only those students who are registered by the education authorities and they suffer from the limitation of not including disabled students of the relevant age who are outside of the education system. However, earlier work (OECD, 1995a), largely confirmed by this data collection round (see Chapter 5), showed that these numbers would be either very small or non-existent since many countries have 100% of students of school age under the aegis of the education authorities.

The data are broken down by categories and presented as proportions of the total numbers of students in pre-primary, primary, lower secondary and upper secondary education. In addition, information is provided on the place or location of these students' education, *i.e.* in regular classes, special classes or special schools, expressed as proportions of the total numbers of students in that category in the particular location.

The data in this chapter have been assembled in the full knowledge of the difficulty of making international comparisons on the basis of national categories. However, at the request of national representatives the analysis is carried out in order to keep touch with the basic data in the form in which it was presented, using terminology that many readers would more readily follow and to provide the context for comparisons made through cross-national categories A, B and C. The method used to make the comparisons is outlined below. Table 2.2 provides background information revealing the inherent difficulty in making international comparisons. First, not all countries use categorical models. Second, the categories that are used are not uniform across countries. Third, the definitions of the categories, when available, vary among countries. It is of course partly for these reasons that the resources model and the cross-national categorisation system have been developed.

Methodology

In order to make the comparisons across the categories provided by countries it is necessary to bring together the different national frameworks that exist. In order to do this, the definitions of the categories were carefully scrutinised and brought together according to the structure of the matrix given in the table in Annex 1. The data classification displayed in this matrix was used to construct the comparative charts, given in the chapter. For example, columns 2 and 3 show national categories covering students who are blind or partially sighted. The data for Belgium (Fl.) shows a "*6x*" in column 2 and a "*6x*" in column 3. The "6" refers to the national category covering students who are blind or partially sighted (see Table 2.2) and the "*x*" indicates that for instance partially sighted students are also included in the category "blind". This means that data cannot be shown separately for these two categories. This is in contrast for instance to France where the data on partially sighted students are contained in their national category 9 and data for blind students in their national category 8. As the two columns reveal few countries keep data on these two groups of students separately and Chart 3.1A has been constructed by bringing together the data for the two groups of students. Comparative charts are only presented if data are available for three or more countries. This means that although data are available for 22 categories only 16 of them allow for international comparisons.

Data on individual categories

Chart 3.1 (A-P) shows the percentages of students in the 16 main national categories of students receiving additional resources to access the curriculum which allow for comparisons across three or more countries. The categories concerning blind and partially sighted students are presented together since the majority of countries do not keep separate data for the two individual categories. This also applies for the data on partially hearing and deaf students, and for that on students with severe and moderate learning problems. Data on aboriginal and indigenous students as well as young offenders data are not analysed because two or less countries provide data on each of these categories. Data on gifted and talented students are not analysed because the educational problems faced by gifted and talented children would appear to be very different from those faced by DDD students.

The percentages are calculated by dividing the number of students in each category by the total number of students in primary and lower secondary education (which are used as proxies for ISCED 1 and 2), with the exception of Belgium (Fl.) which includes upper secondary students (ISCED 3) and Turkey which only includes primary education students (ISCED 1).

The figures are based on full-time study. Data refer to the school year 2000/01, with the exception of Canada (NB) and Greece, where data cover the period 2001/02 and Hungary and Mexico with data from 1999/2000. The figures are based on both public and private institutions.

Charts 3.1A-P are based on the proportions of students in individual categories as a percentage of all students in primary and lower secondary education unless otherwise indicated. They are ranked in ascending order. In some charts, where relevant, the country data are placed in descending order according to the proportions of students educated in regular classes.

Chart 3.1A-P.   **Numbers of students receiving additional resources by nationally classified categories of disability, difficulty and disadvantage and by country, as a percentage of all students in primary and lower secondary education[1] (2001)**

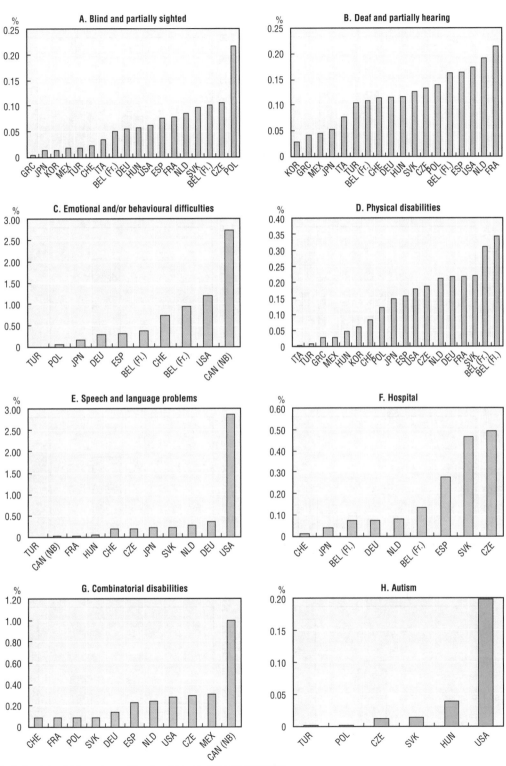

Note: Only includes data which can be readily placed in one of the 16 categories.
1. For France, Germany and Switzerland, data are for the period of compulsory education.

Chart 3.1A-P. **Numbers of students receiving additional resources by nationally classified categories of disability, difficulty and disadvantage and by country, as a percentage of all students in primary and lower secondary education[1] (2001)** *(continued)*

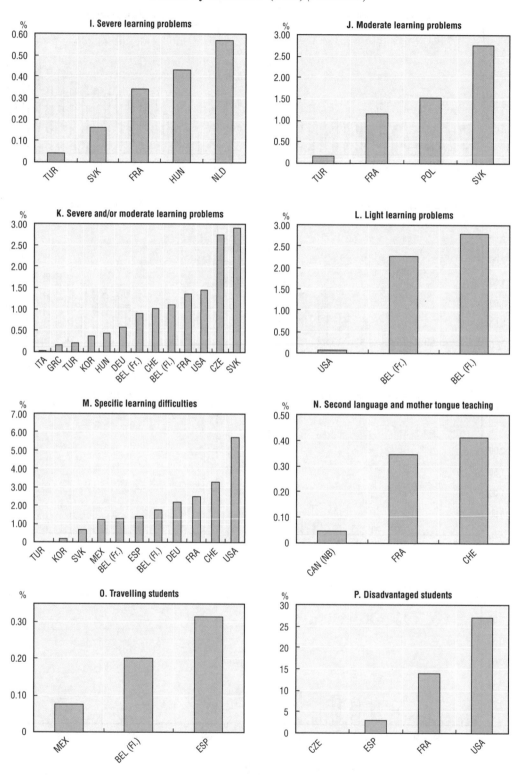

Note: Only includes data which can be readily placed in one of the 16 categories.

1. For France, Germany and Switzerland, data are for the period of compulsory education.

From the point of view of making international comparisons, Chart 3.1 reveals two major issues arising from the natural complexity of the area studied. First, comparison is hampered by the inconsistent use of categories among countries. Only nine, blind and partially sighted (3.1A), deaf and partially hearing (3.1B), emotional and behavioural difficulties (3.1C), physical disabilities (3.1D), speech and language problems (3.1E), hospital (3.1F), combinatorial disabilities (3.1G), severe and moderate learning problems (3.1K) and specific learning difficulties (3.1M) are used by 10 or more countries. The remaining seven are used to varying degrees. All 16 categories are discussed in greater detail in the following sections. Second, close inspection of the individual categories reveals unexpectedly large differences among countries in the proportions of students identified. The information needed to understand these differences is not readily available. Median and inter-quartile ranges are given where 6 or more countries have comparable data. Otherwise, only ranges are provided and an indication given of the different extent of the numbers provided for.

It should be noted that every effort has been made to avoid double counting and that in some cases, proportions may be underestimated because of missing data.

Description by category

Blind and partially sighted

The statistics on the categories covering blind and partially sighted students are treated separately in only a few countries (France, Mexico and Poland) but in most are brought together as a single category which is used for reporting the data here.

As can be seen from Chart 3.1A the proportion of blind and partially sighted students receiving additional resources varies substantially from country to country. The lowest percentage being in Greece (0.005%), and the highest in Poland (0.215%). This means that some countries register in their education statistics proportionally about 43 times more than others. When the highest and the lowest figures are ignored, a large difference remains with the Czech Republic (0.105%) registering nearly seven times as many as Korea and Japan (0.015%). The median percentage of blind and partially sighted students in primary and lower secondary education is 0.06% with an inter-quartile range of 0.02 to 0.08.

Charts 3.2 and 3.3 show where these students are being educated (regular classes, special classes or special schools). A comparison of Charts 3.1A and 3.2 suggests that the different proportions identified are independent of the nature of the placement.

Chart 3.3, on the other hand, shows how variable the placement is among countries.

It shows that eight countries use regular classes, special classes and special schools; the Czech Republic (43.0%, 3.2%, 53.7%), France (52.4%, 10.5%, 37.1%), Italy (95.4%, 0.2%, 4.4%), Japan (9.7%, 11.6%, 78.7%), Korea (2.1%, 19.7%, 78.2%), the Slovak Republic (68.3%, 3.6%, 28.1%), Turkey (31.7%, 4.0%, 64.3%) and the United States (52.2%, 36.1%, 11.7%).

Four countries have a binary system dividing these students between regular classes and special schools: Belgium (Fl.) (39.8%, 60.2%), Germany (26.0%, 74.0%), the Netherlands (64.8%, 35.2%), and Spain (90.7%, 9.3%).

At the extremes, the location of education varies considerably. In Italy, 95% of the blind and partially sighted students are educated in regular classes in contrast to Korea where most of the students are in special schools.

Chart 3.2. **Numbers of blind and partially sighted students by location and by country, as a percentage of all students in primary and lower secondary education**[1, 2, 3]

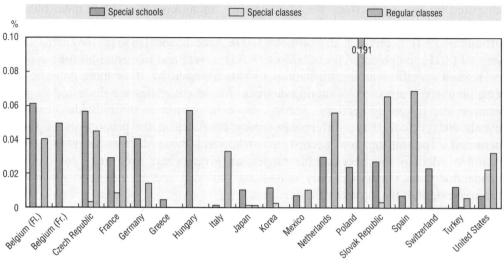

1. In France, Germany and Switzerland the data refer to the period of compulsory education.
2. In special classes data are not applicable in Belgium (Fl.), Belgium (Fr.), the Netherlands and Switzerland; in Greece and Italy data are negligible; in Germany and Spain data are included in specials schools; in Mexico data are included in totals of category A only; in Poland data for specials classes are not available.
3. For regular classes in Belgium (Fl.) data refer to primary, lower secondary and upper secondary; data are not available in Belgium (Fr.), Greece, Hungary and Switzerland; in Korea data for regular classes are negligible.

Chart 3.4 shows how blind and partially sighted students are subdivided according to the various phases of education. The terms pre-primary, primary, lower secondary and upper secondary are used here as proxies for ISCED levels 0, 1, 2 and 3.

Given the nature of the disability making up this category there appears to be little or no consistency across countries in terms of a pattern developing by age.

Chart 3.3. **Numbers of blind and partially sighted students by location and by country, as a percentage of all blind and partially sighted students in primary and lower secondary education**[1, 2, 3, 4]

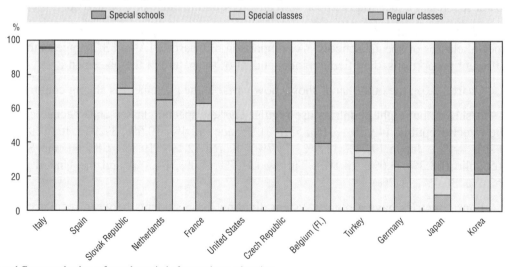

1. In France and Germany the data refer to the period of compulsory education.
2. In Germany and Spain data for special classes are included in special schools.
3. For regular classes in Belgium (Fl.) data refer to primary, lower secondary and upper secondary.
4. In France data for regular classes may be inflated since students from the Ministry of Education only are taken into account here.

Chart 3.4. **Numbers of blind and partially sighted students by phases of education and by country, as a percentage of all students in that phase of education**[1, 2, 3, 4, 5, 6, 7]

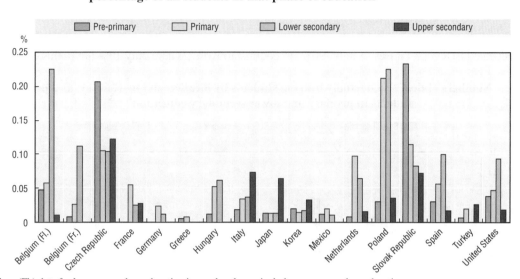

1. In Belgium (Fl.) data for lower secondary education in regular classes include upper secondary education.
2. In Belgium (Fr.) data for lower secondary education in special schools include upper secondary education.
3. In Germany the breakdown by ISCED levels is not available for special schools; therefore data refer to regular classes only.
4. In France data for pre-primary education are not available.
5. In Greece data for lower secondary education include upper secondary education.
6. In Mexico data for upper secondary education are not available.
7. In Turkey data for lower secondary education are not applicable.

Deaf and partially hearing

As for blind and partially sighted students, the statistics gathered on categories covering deaf and partially hearing pupils are treated separately in only a few countries (France, Mexico, the Netherlands and Poland). In most countries, they are treated as a single entity and this method is adopted here.

As can be seen from Chart 3.1B, the proportion of deaf and partially hearing students registered in educational statistics varies substantially from country to country. The lowest percentage being Korea at 0.03% and the highest, France (0.21%). This means that some countries register proportionally 7 times as many as others. If the extremes are ignored, this ratio falls to 4.75, between the Netherlands (0.19%) and Greece (0.04%). The median percentage of deaf and partially hearing students in primary and lower secondary education is 0.12% with an inter-quartile range of 0.08 to 0.16.

Charts 3.5 and 3.6 show where these students are being educated (regular classes, special classes or special schools). A comparison of Charts 3.1B and 3.5 suggests that the different proportions identified are independent of the nature of the placement.

Chart 3.6 on the other hand shows how variable the placement is among countries. It reveals that eight countries divide deaf and hearing impaired pupils among regular classes, special classes and special schools: the Czech Republic (34.3%, 0.3%, 65.4%%), France (45.3%, 9.9%, 44.8%), Italy (96.0%, 1.8%, 2.2%), Japan (23.7%, 17.6%, 58.7%), Korea (17.1%, 15.8%, 67.2%), the Slovak Republic (49.9%, 4.2%, 45.9%), Turkey (23.2%, 11.1%, 65.7%) and the United States (43.3%, 42.5%, 14.2%).

Four countries have a binary system. Regular classes and special schools are used in Belgium (Fl.) (34.5%, 65.5%), Germany (20.2%, 79.8%), the Netherlands (46.1%, 53.9%) and Spain (88.1%, 11.9%).

At the extremes, the location of education varies considerably with the majority being educated in regular classes in Italy (96%) in contrast to Korea where only 17% are in this case.

Chart 3.5.   **Numbers of deaf and partially hearing students by location and by country, as a percentage of all students in primary and lower secondary education**[1, 2, 3, 4]

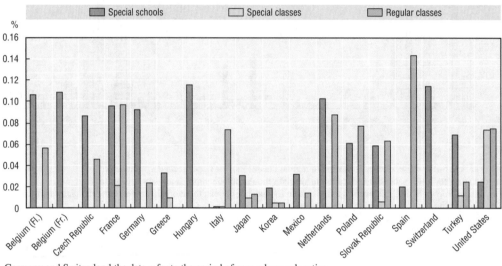

1. In France, Germany and Switzerland the data refer to the period of compulsory education.
2. For special schools in Italy data are negligible.
3. In special classes data are not applicable in Belgium (Fl.), the Netherlands and Switzerland; in the Czech Republic, Greece, Italy and Korea data are negligible; in Germany and Spain data are included in special schools; in Mexico data are included in totals of category A only; in Poland data for specials classes are not available.
4. For regular classes in Belgium (Fl.) data refer to primary, lower secondary and upper secondary; data are not available in Belgium (Fr.), Greece, Hungary and Switzerland; in Japan and Korea data in regular classes are negligible.

Chart 3.6.   **Numbers of deaf and partially hearing students by location and by country, as a percentage of all deaf and partially hearing students in primary and lower secondary education**[1, 2, 3]

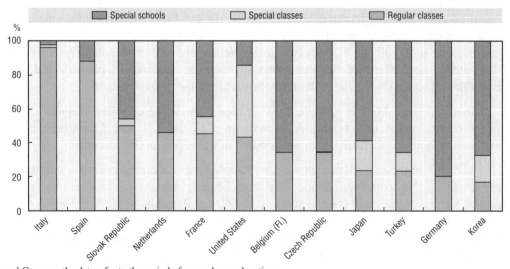

1. In France and Germany the data refer to the period of compulsory education.
2. In Germany and Spain data for special classes are included in special schools.
3. In France data for regular classes may be inflated since students from the Ministry of Education only are taken into account here.

Chart 3.7 shows how deaf and partially hearing students are subdivided according to the various phases of education. As for blind and visually impaired students no consistent patterns over time seem to emerge.

Chart 3.7.   **Numbers of deaf and partially hearing students by phases of education and by country, as a percentage of all students in that phase of education**[1, 2, 3, 4, 5, 6, 7]

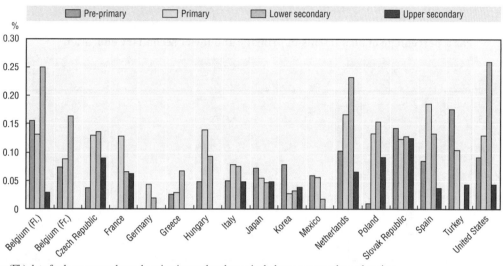

1. In Belgium (Fl.) data for lower secondary education in regular classes include upper secondary education.
2. In Belgium (Fr.) data for lower secondary education in special schools include upper secondary education.
3. In Germany the breakdown by ISCED levels is not available for special schools; therefore data refer to regular classes only.
4. In France data for pre-primary education are not available.
5. In Greece data for lower secondary education include upper secondary education.
6. In Mexico data for upper secondary education are not available.
7. In Turkey data for lower secondary education are not applicable.

Emotional and/or behavioural difficulties

It is of interest to note that given the apparent rise in the numbers of students described as having behaviour difficulties, not all countries use such a category. For those who do, there is evidence for a greater differentiation in terms of location than in the two preceding clusters of categories.

As can be seen from Chart 3.1C the proportion of students with emotional and behavioural difficulties varies substantially from country to country, with Canada (NB) (2.72%) recognising proportionally 2 720 times more than Turkey (0.001%). If the extremes are ignored, the differences are less spectacular with the United States (1.19%) registering 20 times as many as Poland (0.06%). The median percentage of students with emotional and/or behavioural difficulties in primary and lower secondary education is 0.35% with an inter-quartile range of 0.21 to 0.88.

Charts 3.8 and 3.9 show where these students are being educated (regular classes, special classes or special schools). A comparison of Charts 3.1C and 3.8 suggests that the different proportions identified are independent of the nature of the placement.

Chart 3.9 shows the variety of placements offered and indicates that the United States is the only country to use regular classes, special classes and special schools (26.7%, 55.8%, 17.5%).

Five countries use two locations. Regular classes and special schools are used in Belgium (Fl.) (3.7%, 96.3%), Germany (25.6%, 74.4%), Spain (70.0%, 30.0%) and Turkey (94.0%, 6.0%). Japan uses special classes (86.8%) and regular classes (13.2%).

At the extremes, the location of education varies considerably. In Canada (NB) all students with emotional and/or behavioural difficulties are educated in regular classes while in most other countries the majority are in special schools or classes.

Chart 3.8. **Numbers of students with emotional and/or behavioural difficulties by location and by country, as a percentage of all students in primary and lower secondary education[1, 2, 3, 4]**

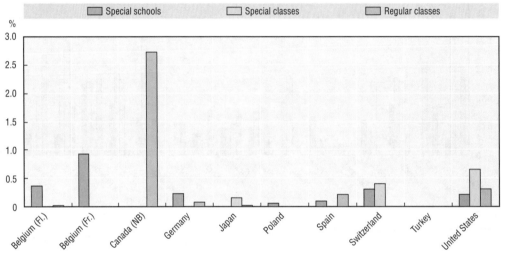

1. In Germany and Switzerland the data refer to the period of compulsory education.
2. For special schools in Canada (NB) and Japan data are not applicable; in Turkey data are negligible.
3. For special classes in Belgium (Fl.), Belgium (Fr.), Canada (NB) and Turkey data are not applicable; in Poland data are not available; in Germany and Spain data are included in special schools.
4. For regular classes in Belgium (Fl.) data refer to primary, lower secondary and upper secondary; data are not available in Belgium (Fr.) and Switzerland; in Turkey data are negligible.

Chart 3.9. **Numbers of students with emotional and/or behavioural difficulties by location and by country, as a percentage of students with emotional and/or behavioural difficulties in primary and lower secondary education[1]**

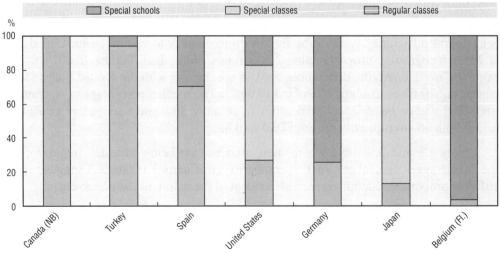

1. In Germany the data refer to the period of compulsory education.

Chart 3.10 shows how students in this category are subdivided according to the various phases of education.

Chart 3.10. **Numbers of students with emotional and/or behavioural difficulties by phases of education and by country, as a percentage of all students in that phase of education**[1, 2, 3, 4, 5, 6, 7, 8]

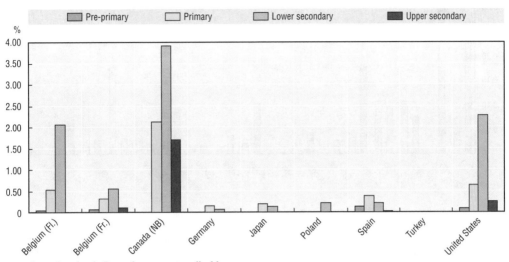

1. For upper secondary education in Japan data are not applicable.
2. For pre-primary education in Canada (NB) and Japan data are not applicable; in Poland data are negligible.
3. In Belgium data for lower secondary education in special schools include upper secondary education.
4. In Germany the breakdown by ISCED levels is not available for special schools; therefore data refer to regular classes only.
5. In Belgium (Fr.) data for lower secondary education in special schools include upper secondary education.
6. For primary education, data are not available in Poland; in Turkey data are negligible.
7. In Turkey data for lower secondary education are not applicable.
8. For upper secondary education data are negligible in Poland.

In most countries where such data are available, the proportion of students with emotional and behavioural difficulties is noticeably higher in lower secondary education than in the other levels. These differences need explaining.

Physical disability

It is readily observable from Chart 3.1D that there is great variation in the proportion of students with physical disabilities in all countries. Belgium (Fl.) (0.343%) has the highest percentage, while the lowest is in Italy (0.001%) which means that proportionally Belgium (Fl.) registers in educational statistics 343 times as many students as Italy. Even if the most extreme countries are not considered, Belgium (Fr.) (0.310%) registers 40 times more than Turkey (0.008%). The median percentage of physically disabled students in primary and lower secondary education is 0.15% with an inter-quartile range of 0.05 to 0.21.

Charts 3.11 and 3.12 show where these students are being educated (regular classes, special classes or special schools). A comparison of Charts 3.1D and 3.11 suggests that the different proportions identified are independent of the nature of the placement.

Chart 3.12 on the other hand, shows how variable the placement is among countries.

As shown in Chart 3.12, six countries use all three locations, regular classes, special classes and special schools; the Czech Republic (57.5%, 2.5%, 40.1%), France (49.0%, 6.9%, 44.1%), Japan (0.1%, 17.3%, 82.6%), Korea (10.5%, 28.1%, 61.4%), the Slovak Republic (82.1%, 3.1%, 14.8%) and the United States (47.3%, 47.2%, 5.5%).

Chart 3.11. **Numbers of students with physical disabilities by location and by country, as a percentage of all students in primary and lower secondary education**[1, 2, 3, 4]

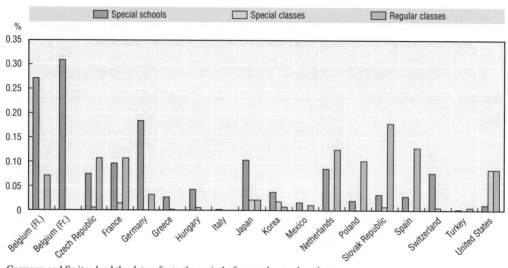

1. In France, Germany and Switzerland the data refer to the period of compulsory education.
2. For special schools, in Italy and Turkey data are negligible.
3. In special classes, data are not applicable in Belgium (Fl.), Belgium (Fr.), the Netherlands, Switzerland and Turkey; in the Czech Republic, Greece and Italy data are negligible; in Germany and Spain data are included in special schools; in Mexico data are included in totals of category A only; in Poland data for special classes are not available.
4. For regular classes in Belgium (Fr.), Greece, Italy and Switzerland data are not available; in Belgium (Fl.) data refer to primary, lower secondary and upper secondary.

Chart 3.12. **Numbers of students with physical disabilities by location and by country, as a percentage of all students with physical disabilities in primary and lower secondary education**[1, 2]

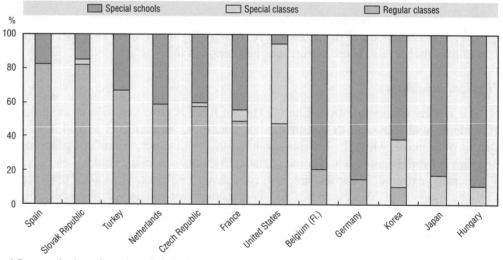

1. In France and Germany the data refer to the period of compulsory education.
2. For regular classes in Belgium (Fl.) data refer to primary, lower secondary and upper secondary.

Five countries have systems which distribute these students between regular classes and special schools: Belgium (Fl.) (20.9%, 79.1%), Germany (15.0%, 85.0%), the Netherlands (59.0%, 41.0%), Spain (82.2%, 17.8%) and Turkey (66.8%, 33.2%). One country uses special classes and special schools, Hungary (10.9%, 89.1%).

At the extremes the location of education varies considerably. Countries can be distributed into two groups: one where the majority of students are educated in regular classes, the other where less than a fourth of them are. In the first group, the Slovak Republic and Spain are at the top of the scale with more than 80%.

Chart 3.13 shows how students in this category are subdivided according to the various phases of education. Again no consistent trend emerges. It can be observed that the percentages for Belgium (both Flemish and French communities) during lower secondary education are substantially greater in contrast both to the primary level in those countries and also in comparison to other countries.

Chart 3.13. **Numbers of students with physical disabilities by phases of education and by country, as a percentage of all students in that phase of education** [1, 2, 3, 4, 5, 6]

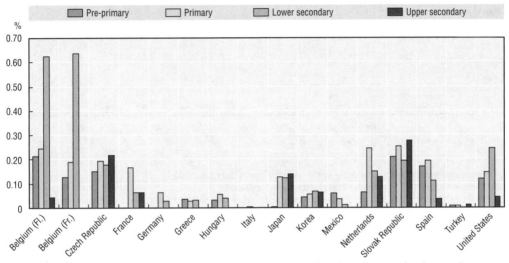

1. In Germany, the breakdown by ISCED levels is not available for special needs; therefore data refer to regular classes only.
2. In Belgium (Fr.) and Greece data for lower secondary education in special schools include upper secondary education.
3. For pre-primary education in France data are not available; in Italy and Japan data are negligible.
4. For primary education in Italy data are negligible.
5. For lower secondary education in Italy data are negligible; in Turkey data are not applicable.
6. For upper secondary education in Italy and Mexico data are not available.

Speech and language problems

As can be seen from Chart 3.1E the percentages of students registered with speech and language problems also vary substantially from country to country, the lowest percentage being in Turkey (0.006%) and the highest in the United States (2.86%). This means that some countries register proportionally almost 500 times as many as others. If the extremes are ignored, the variation is reduced with Germany (0.37%) registering 15.7 times more than Canada (NB) (0.02%). Nonetheless, the differences remain substantial. The median percentage of students with speech and language problems in primary and lower secondary education is 0.18% with an inter-quartile range of 0.05 to 0.24.

Charts 3.14 and 3.15 show where these students are being educated (regular classes, special classes or special schools). A comparison of Charts 3.1E and 3.14 suggests that the different proportions identified are independent of the nature of the placement.

Chart 3.15 on the other hand, shows how variable the placement is among countries showing that three countries use regular classes, special classes and special schools: the

Czech Republic (35.6%, 3.8%, 60.6%), the Slovak Republic (74.9%, 6.1%, 19.0%) and the United States (85.9%, 13.2%, 0.9%).

Chart 3.14. **Numbers of students with speech and language problems by location and by country, as a percentage of all students in primary and lower secondary education**[1, 2, 3, 4]

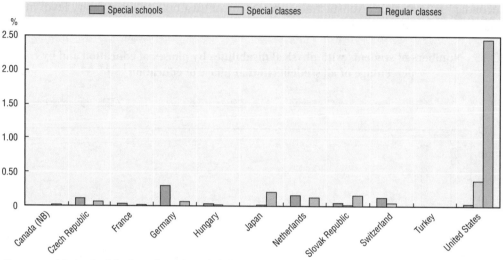

1. In France, Germany and Switzerland the data refer to the period of compulsory education.
2. For special schools in Canada (NB), Japan and Turkey data are not applicable.
3. For special classes in Canada (NB), France, the Netherlands and Turkey data are not applicable; in Germany data are included in special schools.
4. For regular classes in Hungary and Switzerland data are not available.

Chart 3.15. **Numbers of students with speech and language problems by location and by country, as a percentage of all students with speech and language problems in primary and lower secondary education**[1]

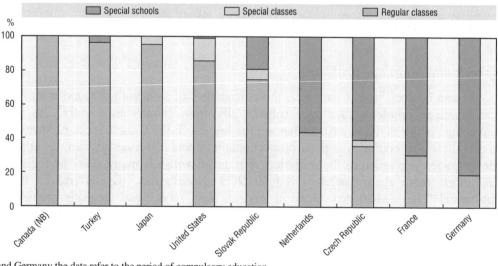

1. In France and Germany the data refer to the period of compulsory education.

Five countries use only two locations. Regular classes and special schools are used in France (30.3%, 69.7%), Germany (19.1%, 80.9%), the Netherlands (43.6%, 56.4%) and Turkey (96.1%, 3.9%). Japan uses special classes (95.1%) and regular classes (4.9%).

In Canada (NB) all students in this category are in regular classes while in Germany and France they are nearly all in special schools. Two different approaches can be identified, one with the countries where the majority of students are educated in special schools, another where more than 75% of the students are in regular classes.

Chart 3.16 shows how students in this category are subdivided according to the various phases of education.

Chart 3.16. **Numbers of students with speech and language problems by phases of education and by country, as a percentage of all students in that phase of education**[1, 2, 3, 4, 5]

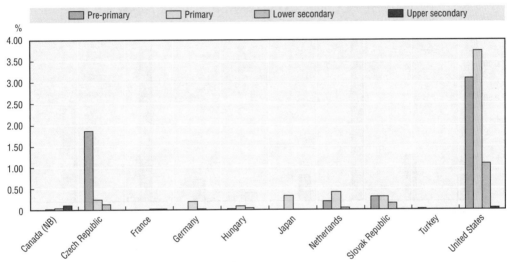

1. In Germany, the breakdown by ISCED levels is not available; therefore data refer to regular classes only.
2. For pre-primary education in Canada (NB) and Japan data are not applicable; in France data are not available.
3. For primary education in France data are not available.
4. For lower secondary education in Turkey data are not applicable; in Japan data are negligible.
5. For upper secondary education in Hungary and the Netherlands data are not available; in Turkey data are negligible.

Eight countries provided data allowing for a breakdown by ISCED levels. As with most of the other categories this data show no consistent pattern between proportions of students identified and ISCED level.

Hospital

As can be seen from Chart 3.1F, the percentage of students registered as receiving education while hospitalised varies substantially from country to country; the lowest percentage being in Switzerland (0.011%) and the highest in the Czech Republic (0.489%). This means that some countries register proportionally 43 times as many as others. However if the extremes are ignored the differences are considerably reduced, with the Slovak Republic hospitalising almost seven times more than Belgium (Fl.). The median percentage of these students in primary and lower secondary education is 0.07% with an inter-quartile range of 0.07 to 0.28.

Charts 3.17 and 3.18 show where these students are being educated (regular classes, special classes or special schools).

Chart 3.18 on the other hand shows how variable the placement is among countries. The chart shows that four countries use one location only, either special schools or regular schools. The data thus confirm the wide variety of provision which is used for these students. In Belgium (Fl.) students are in the so-called "hospital schools" for a limited period of time; in the meantime they remain also registered in their usual place of education. Countries who use two locations are the Netherlands which places these students in regular classes (16.3%) and special schools (83.7%), and the Slovak Republic which uses special schools and special classes with 97.6% of the students in special schools. Japan uses all three locations, special schools (62.7%), special classes (36.8%), and regular classes (0.5%).

Chart 3.17. **Numbers of students in hospitals by location, as a percentage of all students in primary and lower secondary education**[1, 2, 3, 4]

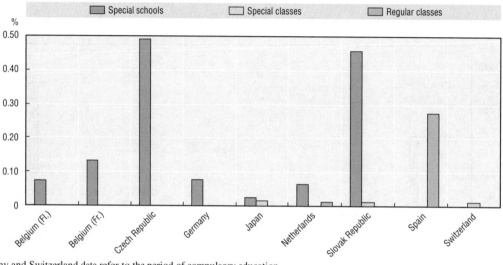

1. In Germany and Switzerland data refer to the period of compulsory education.
2. For special schools in Spain and Switzerland data are not applicable; in Belgium (Fl.) data refer to primary, lower secondary and upper secondary education.
3. For special classes in Belgium (Fl.), Belgium (Fr.), the Czech Republic, the Netherlands and Spain data are not applicable; in Germany data are included in special schools.
4. For regular classes in Belgium (Fl.) and the Czech Republic data are not applicable; in Belgium (Fr.) and Switzerland data are not available.

Chart 3.18. **Numbers of students in hospitals by location and by country, as a percentage of all students in hospitals in primary and lower secondary education**[1]

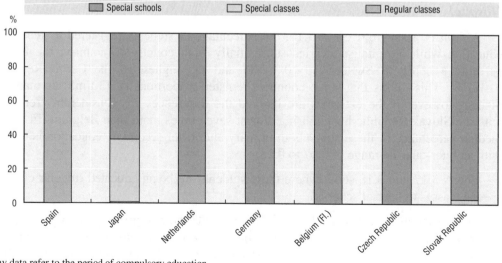

1. In Germany data refer to the period of compulsory education.

Chart 3.19 shows how students in this category are subdivided according to the various phases of education. No particular pattern emerges.

Chart 3.19. **Numbers of students in hospitals by phases of education and by country, as a percentage of all students in that phase of education[1, 2, 3]**

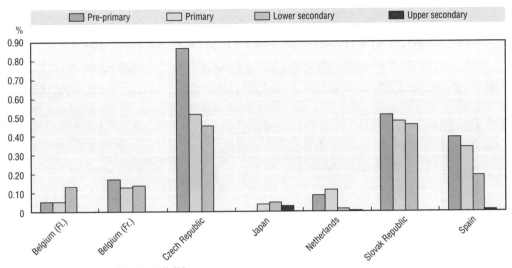

1. For pre-primary education in Japan data are negligible.
2. In Belgium (Fl.) and Belgium (Fr.) data for lower secondary education in special schools include upper secondary education.
3. For upper secondary education in the Czech Republic data are not applicable.

Combinatorial disabilities

Combinatorial disabilities is a term that has been coined by the Secretariat to avoid the confusion in an earlier monograph (OECD, 2000b) over the use of "multiple disability" which in the United States is a legally defined category but which is too precisely defined to cover the range of students included in the "combinatorial" category used here.

Chart 3.1G shows that again the proportions of students in this category vary substantially from country to country. The lowest percentages being found in France, Poland, the Slovak Republic and Switzerland (0.09%) and the highest in Canada (NB) (1.00%). This means that some countries register in educational statistics proportionally 11 times as many as others do. If the extremes are ignored, the differences are substantially reduced, with Mexico (0.31%) registering 2.2 times more than Germany (0.14). The median percentage of students with combinatorial disabilities in primary and lower secondary education is 0.22% with an inter-quartile range of 0.09 to 0.29.

Charts 3.20 and 3.21 show where these students are being educated (regular classes, special classes or special schools). A comparison of Charts 3.1G and 3.20 suggests that the different proportions identified are independent of the nature of the placement.

Chart 3.21, on the other hand, shows how variable the placement is among countries and shows that two countries have systems which use regular classes, special classes and special schools: the Czech Republic (30.8%, 5.5%, 63.7%), and the United States (12.8%, 62.8%, 24.4%).

Three countries use only two locations, regular classes and special schools: Germany (66.0%, 34.0%), the Netherlands (9.9%, 90.1%) and Spain (47.6%, 52.4%). France and the Slovak Republic place all of these students into special schools.

It is noteworthy that in Canada (NB) these very impaired students are all educated in regular classes.

Chart 3.20. **Numbers of students with combinatorial disabilities in primary and lower secondary by location and by country, as a percentage of all students in primary and lower secondary[1, 2, 3, 4]**

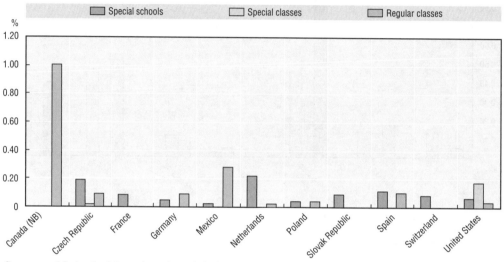

1. In France, Germany and Switzerland data refer to the period of compulsory education.
2. For special schools in Canada (NB) data are not applicable.
3. For special classes in Canada (NB), France, the Netherlands and Switzerland data are not applicable; in Germany and Spain data are included in special schools; in Mexico data are included in totals of category A only; in Poland data for special classes are not available.
4. For regular classes in France data are not applicable; in Switzerland data are not available.

Chart 3.21. **Numbers of students with combinatorial disabilities by location and by country, as a percentage of all students with combinatorial disabilities in primary and lower secondary education[1]**

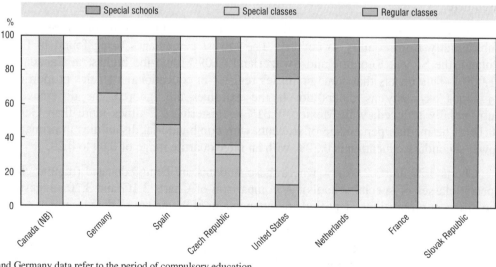

1. In France and Germany data refer to the period of compulsory education.

Chart 3.22 shows how students in this category are subdivided according to the various phases of education. In seven countries out of ten, a peak is reached at the primary level of education.

Chart 3.22. **Numbers of students with combinatorial disabilities by phases of education and by country, as a percentage of all students in that phase of education[1, 2, 3]**

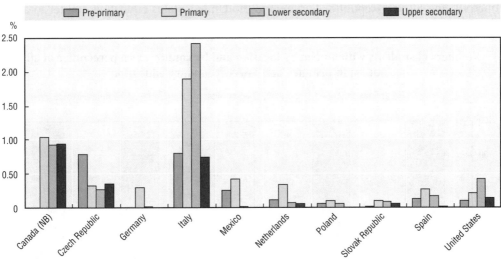

1. In Germany, the breakdown by ISCED levels is not available for special schools; therefore data refer to regular classes only.
2. For pre-primary education in Canada (NB) data are not applicable.
3. For upper secondary education in Mexico data are not applicable; in Poland data are not available.

Autism

The worldwide interest in the topic of autism is revealed in the growing number of countries who use this as a clear category to gather statistics. Chart 3.1H shows the variation between them. The United States stand out with students with autism receiving additional resources representing 0.20% of the school population, 100 times more than Turkey and Poland (0.002%). With the extremes removed, Hungary (0.039%) identifies 3 times more than the Czech Republic (0.013%). The median percentage of students with autism in primary and lower secondary education is 0.01% with an inter-quartile range of 0.004 to 0.03.

Chart 3.23. **Numbers of students with autism in primary and lower secondary by location and by country, as a percentage of all students in primary and lower secondary education[1, 2]**

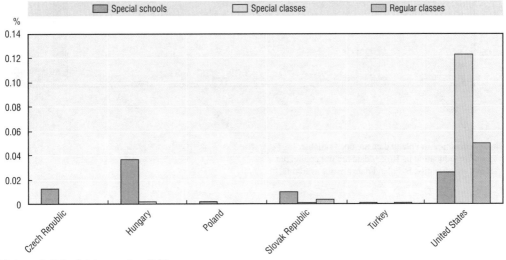

1. For special classes in Poland data are not available.
2. For regular classes in the Czech Republic data are not applicable; in Poland data are not available.

Charts 3.23 and 3.24 show where these students are being educated. Special provisions (either special schools or classes) are clearly preferred although three countries, the Slovak Republic, Turkey and the United States educate a quarter to a third in regular classes.

Chart 3.24. **Numbers of students with autism by location and by country, as a percentage of all students with autism in primary and lower secondary education**

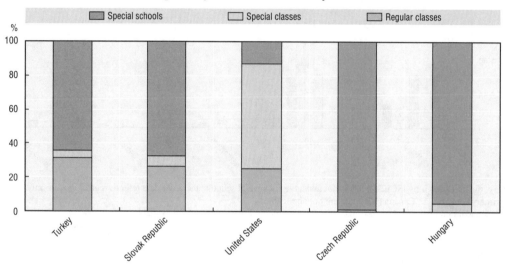

Chart 3.25. **Numbers of students with autism by phases of education and by country, as a percentage of all students in that phase of education[1, 2, 3]**

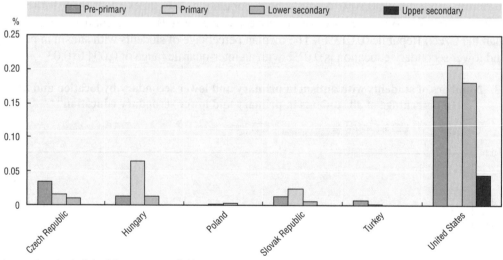

1. For pre-primary education in Poland data are not available.
2. For lower secondary education in Turkey data are not applicable.
3. For upper secondary education in Poland data are not available.

Chart 3.25 shows how students in this category are subdivided according to the various phases of education. If the pre-primary period is ignored a more consistent trend emerges with fewer students identified in the older age groups. A most noticeable aspect is the much greater proportion of students classified with autism in the Unites States across all phases of education.

Severe learning problems

Five countries keep statistics for students with severe learning problems as Chart 3.1I shows.

As can be seen from Chart 3.1I the proportion of students registered with severe learning problems varies substantially from country to country; the lowest percentage being in Turkey (0.04%) and the highest in the Netherlands (0.57%). This means that Netherlands registers proportionally 13 times as many as Turkey. However, if the extremes are ignored, the differences are substantially reduced with Hungary (0.43%) registering 2.7 times more than the Slovak Republic (0.16%).

Charts 3.26 and 3.27 show where these students are being educated – regular classes, special classes or special schools.

Chart 3.27 shows that special schools are undoubtedly the preferred provision for students with severe learning problems. In France and in the Slovak Republic they are the only form of provision with the Netherlands close behind with 97.9% in special schools and only 2.1% in regular classes. Only Turkey makes use of special classes.

Chart 3.26. **Numbers of students with severe learning problems by location and by country, as a percentage of all students in primary and lower secondary education[1, 2, 3]**

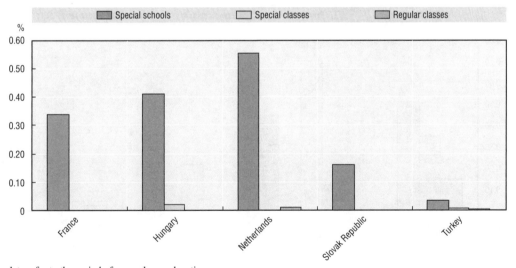

1. In France data refer to the period of compulsory education.
2. For special classes in France and the Netherlands data are not applicable.
3. For regular classes in France data are not applicable; in Hungary data are not available; in Turkey data are negligible.

Chart 3.27. **Numbers of students with severe learning problems by location and by country, as a percentage of all students with severe learning problems in primary and lower secondary education**[1]

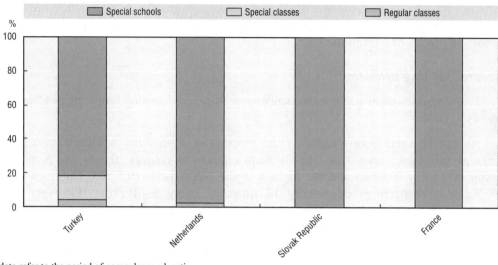

1. In France data refer to the period of compulsory education.

Chart 3.28 shows how students in this category are subdivided according to the various phases of education. Again, no particular pattern appears.

Chart 3.28. **Numbers of students with severe learning problems by phases of education and by country, as a percentage of all students in that phase of education**[1]

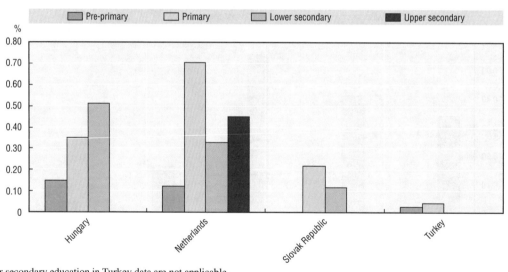

1. For lower secondary education in Turkey data are not applicable.

Moderate learning problems

As can be seen from Chart 3.1J the proportions of students experiencing moderate learning problems vary substantially from country to country; the lowest percentage being in Turkey (0.17%) and the highest in the Slovak Republic (2.75%). This means that the Slovak Republic registers proportionally 16 times as many as Turkey.

Chart 3.29 shows where these students are being educated (regular classes, special classes or special schools). A comparison of Charts 3.1J and 3.29 suggests that the more students identified the greater the use of special schools.

Chart 3.30 shows that data on location of education are only available for three countries and they all use all three locations – regular classes, special classes and special schools. However, their relative use varies greatly. Turkish students with moderate learning problems are predominantly educated in regular classes (52.5%). The French system tends to favour special classes (49.7%) while in the Slovak Republic 79.8% are in special schools.

Chart 3.29. **Numbers of students with moderate learning problems by location and by country, as a percentage of all students in primary and lower secondary education**[1, 2]

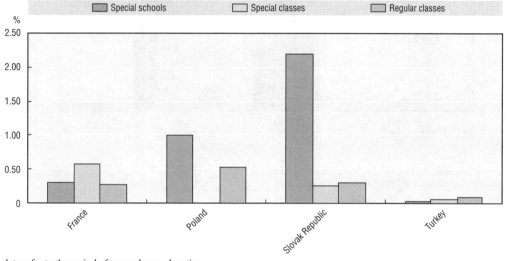

1. In France data refer to the period of compulsory education.
2. For special classes in Poland data are not available.

Chart 3.30. **Numbers of students with moderate learning problems by location and by country, as a percentage of all students with moderate learning problems in primary and lower secondary education**[1]

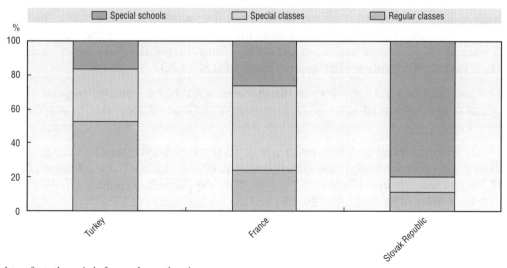

1. In France data refer to the period of compulsory education.

Four countries provided data allowing for a breakdown of students across pre-primary, primary, lower secondary and upper secondary (Chart 3.31). As with many other categories this data show no consistent pattern between proportions of students identified and levels of education.

Chart 3.31. **Numbers of students with moderate learning problems by phases of education and by country, as a percentage of all students in that phase of education[1,2]**

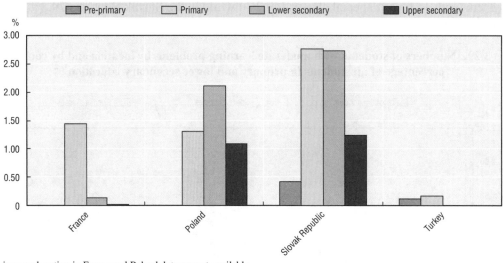

1. For pre-primary education in France and Poland data are not available.
2. For lower secondary education in Turkey data are not applicable.

Severe and/or moderate learning problems

The previous two sections showed the limited available data on severe and moderate learning problems, separately. Ten countries however provide data covering both categories as a whole.

Chart 3.1K shows the proportions of resourced students with severe and/or moderate learning problems by country. The variations across countries are considerable. Italy presents the lowest percentage (0.01%), and the Slovak Republic the highest (2.91%). This means that the Slovak Republic registers proportionally more than 200 times as many as Italy. Even when ignoring the extremes the variation is considerable, the Czech Republic (2.74%) registering 16 times more than Greece (0.17%). The median percentage of students with severe and/or moderate problems in primary and lower secondary education is 0.90% with an inter-quartile range of 0.36 to 1.37.

Chart 3.32 and 3.33 show where these students are being educated (regular classes, special classes or special schools). A comparison of Charts 3.1K and 3.32 suggests that the different proportions identified are independent of the nature of the placement.

Six countries presented here make use of all three locations (regular classes, special classes and special schools): the Czech Republic (0.5%, 3.8%, 95.7%), France (17.8%, 37.3%, 44.9%), Korea (3.6%, 47.7%, 48.8%), the Slovak Republic (10.4%, 8.7%, 80.9%), Turkey (42.8%, 27.8%, 29.4%) and the United States (13.7%, 81.6%, 4.7%). In none of these is regular class the principal type of provision.

Germany uses almost exclusively special schools (97.3%) with only 2.7% of the students educated in regular classes.

In Belgium (both communities), registered students with severe and/or moderate learning problems are all educated in special schools.

Chart 3.32. **Numbers of students with severe and/or moderate learning problems by location and by country, as a percentage of all students in primary and lower secondary education**[1, 2, 3]

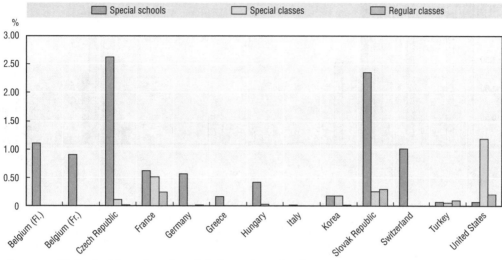

1. In France, Germany and Switzerland data refer to the period of compulsory education.
2. For special classes in Belgium (Fl.), Belgium (Fr.) and Switzerland data are not applicable; in Greece and Italy data are negligible; in Germany data for special classes are included in special schools.
3. For regular classes in Belgium (Fr.) data are not applicable; in Greece, Hungary, Italy and Switzerland data are not available; in Belgium (Fl.) data are negligible.

Chart 3.33. **Numbers of students with severe and/or moderate learning problems by location and by country, as a percentage of all students with severe and/or moderate learning problems in primary and lower secondary education**[1]

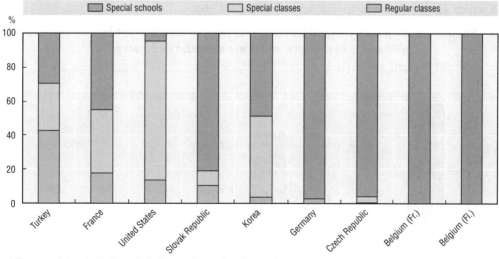

1. In France and Germany data refer to the period of compulsory education.

Chart 3.34 reveals the proportions of these students across pre-primary, primary, lower secondary and upper secondary. There is no clear trend, although the proportion of these students in lower secondary education seems notably elevated in Belgium (Fl. and Fr.) and in the United States.

Chart 3.34. **Numbers of students with severe and/or moderate learning problems by phases of education and by country, as a percentage of all students in that phase of education**[1, 2, 3, 4, 5]

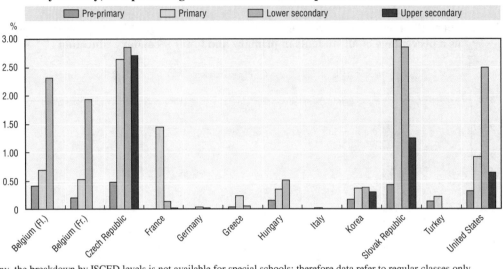

1. In Germany, the breakdown by ISCED levels is not available for special schools; therefore data refer to regular classes only.
2. For pre-primary education in Germany data are not applicable; in France data are not available.
3. For lower secondary education in Turkey data are not applicable; in Italy data are negligible.
4. In Belgium (Fl.), Belgium (Fr.) and Greece data for lower secondary education in special schools include upper secondary education.
5. For upper secondary education in Italy data are negligible.

Light learning problems

In general, little data was provided for this category and Chart 3.1L shows the data from the countries that did. They indicate large variations in the proportions of students resourced. Proportionally, Belgium (Fl.) resources 40 times more students with light learning problems than the United States (Chart 3.35). In addition, the location of education varies considerably among the countries providing data, with the United States educating half of these students in regular classes contrasting with Belgium (Fl. and Fr.) in which almost all are in special schools (Chart 3.36).

Chart 3.35. **Numbers of students with light learning problems by location and by country, as a percentage of all students in primary and lower secondary education**[1, 2, 3, 4]

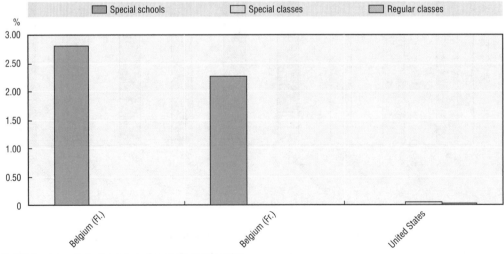

1. In the United States data refer to the period of compulsory education.
2. For special schools in the United States data are negligible.
3. For special classes in Belgium (Fl.) and Belgium (Fr.) data are not applicable.
4. For regular classes in Belgium (Fr.) data are not applicable; in Belgium (Fl.) data are negligible.

Chart 3.36. **Numbers of students with light learning problems by location and by country, as a percentage of all students with light learning problems in primary and lower secondary education**[1, 2]

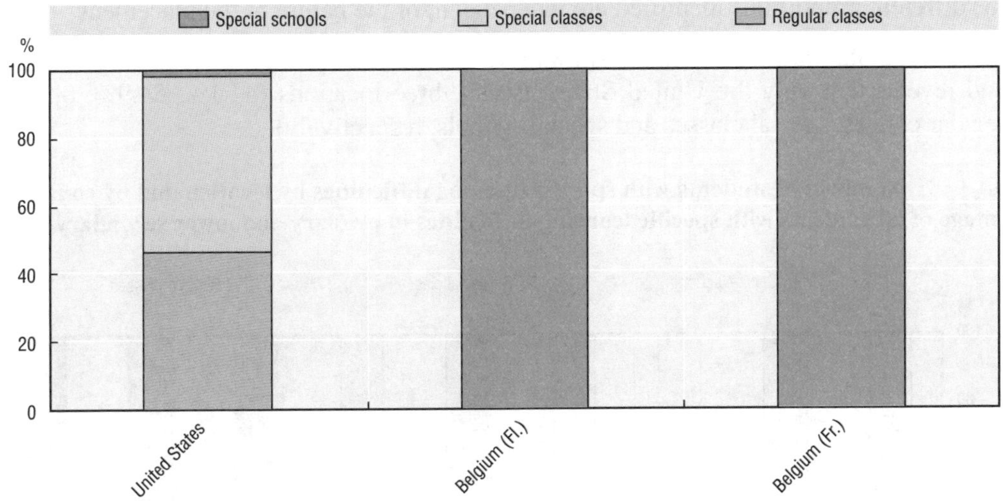

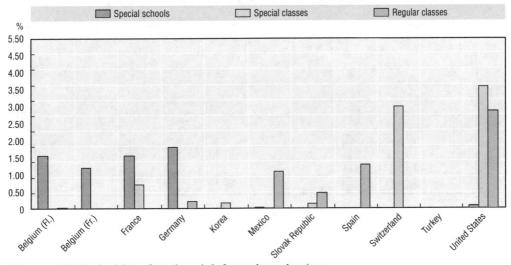

1. In the United States data refer to the period of compulsory education.
2. For regular classes in Belgium (Fl.) data refer to primary, lower secondary and upper secondary education.

Specific learning difficulties

Chart 3.1M shows that, as for many of the other categories, there is substantial variation among countries in the proportions of students categorised with specific learning difficulties. The highest proportion is in the United States who register proportionally 600 times as many as Turkey (0.01%). Even if the extremes are removed Switzerland (3.30%) still identifies 18 times the students in Korea (0.18%). The median percentage of students with specific learning difficulties in primary and lower secondary education is 1.41% with an inter-quartile range of 0.92 to 2.34.

Chart 3.37. **Numbers of students with specific learning difficulties by location and by country, as a percentage of all students in primary and lower secondary education**[1, 2, 3, 4]

1. In France, Germany and Switzerland data refer to the period of compulsory education.
2. For special schools in Korea, Spain and Switzerland data are not applicable; in Turkey data are negligible.
3. For special classes in Belgium (Fr.), Spain and Turkey data are not applicable; in Mexico data are included in totals of category A only; in Germany data are included in special schools.
4. For regular schools in Belgium (Fr.) and France data are not applicable; in Switzerland data are not available.

Charts 3.37 and 3.38 show where these students are being educated (regular classes, special classes or special schools). A comparison of Charts 3.1M and 3.37 suggests that the different proportions identified are independent of the nature of the placement.

Chart 3.38, on the other hand, shows how variable the placement is among countries and reveals that only the United States use all three locations (44.1%, 54.9%, 0.9% in regular classes, special classes and special schools, respectively).

Chart 3.38. **Numbers of students with specific learning difficulties by location and by country, as a percentage of all students with specific learning difficulties in primary and lower secondary education**[1]

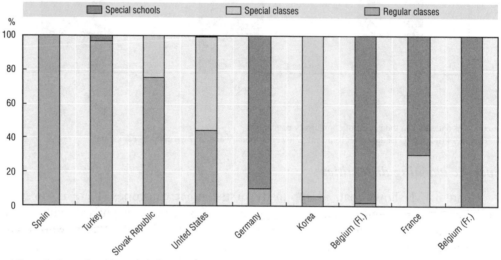

1. In France and Germany data refer to the period of compulsory education.

Chart 3.39. **Numbers of students with specific learning difficulties by phases of education and by country, as a percentage of all students in that phase of education**[1, 2, 3, 4]

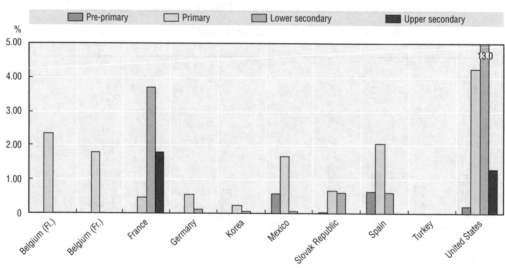

1. In Germany, the breakdown by ISCED levels is not available for special schools; therefore data refer to regular classes only.
2. For pre-primary education in Belgium (Fl.), Belgium (Fr.), France and Turkey data are not applicable; in Korea data are negligible.
3. For lower secondary education in Belgium (Fl.), Belgium (Fr.) and Turkey data are not applicable.
4. For upper secondary education in Belgium (Fl.) and Belgium (Fr.) data are not applicable; in Mexico data are not available; in Turkey data are negligible.

Six countries use two locations. Belgium (Fl.) (98.1%) and Germany (89.7%) use mostly special schools, the rest following regular classes. Korea and the Slovak Republic make use of regular classes and special classes, but in opposite ways. In Korea, special classes receive 94.1% of the students while in the Slovak Republic 75% are in regular classes. France uses both special schools (69.4%) and special classes. Turkey uses special schools (3.3%) and regular classes (96.7%).

The two remaining countries use a single type of provision. In Spain all of these students are in regular classes while in Belgium (Fr.) they are all in special schools.

Chart 3.39 reveals the proportions of these students across pre-primary, primary, lower secondary and upper secondary education. In all countries represented here, with the exception of France and the United States where the proportion is very elevated at the lower secondary level, the primary level of education is the one with the highest proportion of resourced students with specific learning difficulties.

Additional categories related to disadvantage

The analysis presented in the following section is based on data on national categories related to disadvantage where common categories could be provided for making international comparisons. Three of these emerged covering: second language and mother tongue students; travelling students; and disadvantaged students.

Second language and mother tongue teaching

This category brings together data on students who do not speak the national language of instruction (second language) with those receiving courses on mother tongue teaching. These courses allow foreign students to maintain their mother tongue competences. They are brought together since some countries do not separate out these two types of provision in their statistical returns.

Chart 3.40. **Numbers of second language and mother tongue teaching students by location and by country, as a percentage of all students in primary and lower secondary education**[1, 2, 3, 4]

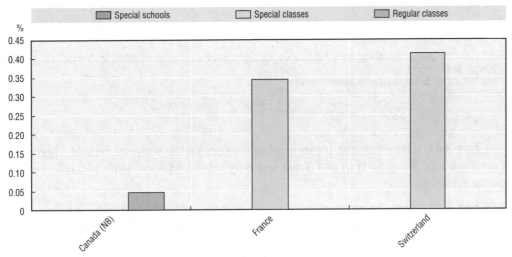

1. In France and Switzerland data refer to the period of compulsory education.
2. For special schools in Canada (NB), France and Switzerland data are not applicable.
3. For special classes in Canada (NB) data are not applicable.
4. For regular classes in France data are not applicable; in Switzerland data are not available.

Chart 3.1N shows the countries providing data for this category. They indicate large variations in the proportions of students resourced. Switzerland (0.41%) resources proportionally nine times more than in Canada (NB) (0.05%).

Chart 3.40 shows that the location of education only varies between regular classes and special schools. Canada (NB) uses only regular classes while France and Switzerland use exclusively special classes.

The proportions of these students across pre-primary, primary, lower secondary and upper secondary education can be calculated for only two countries, with no consistent pattern emerging between the proportions of students identified and ISCED levels.

Travelling students

Chart 3.1O shows the countries providing data for this category with Spain (0.32%) resourcing proportionally 4 times as many students as Mexico (0.08%).

Chart 3.41. **Numbers of travelling students by location and by country, as a percentage of all students in primary and lower secondary education**[1, 2, 3]

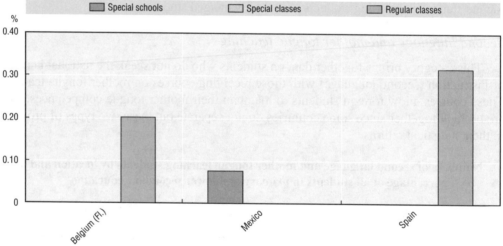

1. In Belgium (Fl.) data for special schools and special classes are not applicable. Education for travelling students is only organised in regular classes at pre-primary and primary levels.
2. In Mexico data for special classes and regular classes are not available.
3. In Spain data for special classes are not applicable.

Chart 3.41 shows that the location of education varies between regular classes and special schools. Belgium (Fl.) and Spain use only regular classes while Mexico uses only special schools.

Chart 3.42 shows the proportions of these students across pre-primary, primary, lower secondary and upper secondary with too little data being available to allow for further comments.

Chart 3.42. **Numbers of travelling students by phases of education and by country, as a percentage of all students in that phase of education[1, 2, 3]**

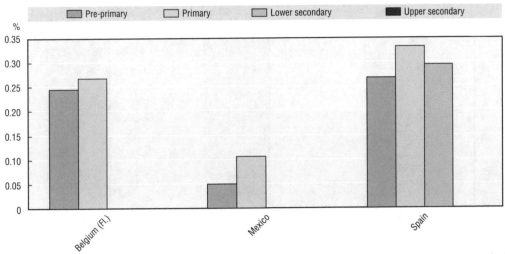

1. In Belgium (Fl.) data for special schools and special classes are not applicable. Education for travelling students is only organised in regular classes at pre-primary and primary levels.
2. For lower secondary education in Mexico data are not available.
3. For upper secondary education in Mexico data are not applicable.

Disadvantaged students

Chart 3.1P shows the countries providing data for this category. They indicate large variations in the proportions of students resourced. The United States (26.97%) resource proportionally about 300 times more than the Czech Republic (0.09%). If the extremes are removed the difference still remains large with France (13.94%) resourcing almost 5 times that of Spain (2.97%).

Chart 3.43. **Numbers of disadvantaged students by location and by country, as a percentage of all students in primary and lower secondary education[1, 2, 3, 4, 5]**

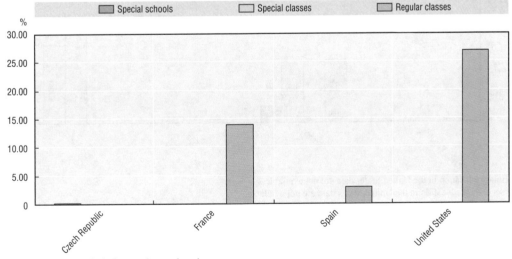

1. In France data refer to the period of compulsory education.
2. Data for the United States are estimates.
3. For special schools in France, Spain and the United States data are not applicable.
4. For special classes data are not applicable in any country.
5. For regular classes in the Czech Republic data are not available.

Chart 3.44. **Numbers of disadvantaged students by location and by country, as a percentage of all disadvantaged students in primary and lower secondary education**[1]

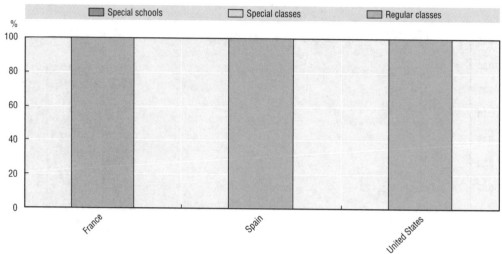

1. In France data refer to the period of compulsory education.

Charts 3.43 and 3.44 show that France, Spain and the United States only use regular classes. In the Czech Republic some of these students are in special schools.[1]

Chart 3.45. **Numbers of disadvantaged students by phases of education and by country, as a percentage of all students in that phase of education**[1,2]

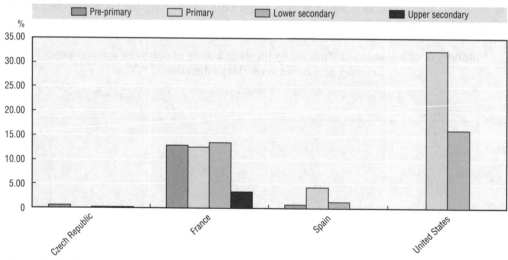

1. For pre-primary education in the United States data are not available.
2. For upper secondary education in the United States data are not available.

1. The data from the Czech Republic include "socially disadvantaged children in preparatory classes and regular schools". These category 11 students are educated in special schools.

Chart 3.45 shows the proportions of these students across pre-primary, primary, lower secondary and upper secondary. There seems to be no evident pattern between the proportions of students identified and ISCED levels.

Conclusions

This chapter has considered the data based on the national categories used to provide additional resources for children and students having difficulties accessing the curriculum – as supplied by participating countries. It has looked at the proportions registered in educational statistics by category, by location of education, and by ISCED level. The data show substantial variation in categories used by countries and in the country prevalence rates for the school years covering pre-primary, primary, lower secondary and upper secondary education. Furthermore, the location of education – regular schools, special classes, or special schools – varies greatly from country to country. For almost all categories at the extremes the education experiences of similar students would be very different in different countries. For instance, in one they might be educated in regular classes while in another they may be fully segregated from mainstream education.

Because of the different definitions in use of national categories for these students the present study has adopted a simplified tri-partite cross-national categorisation, referred to as A, B and C within the context of a resources model which has been outlined in previous chapters. The following chapters use this framework to describe the remainder of the data gathered by the quantitative part of the instrument.

General notes

Canada (NB): Note that for New Brunswick the data have been submitted by District 18 only. School District 18 is one of 13 school districts (9 anglophone, 4 francophone) that organises education in the Province of New Brunswick. The total student population is approximately 120 600 (84 575 anglophone, 36 025 francophone). School District 18 has 12 832 students served by over 1 200 employees. Pre-primary students are not part of the public school system.

Finland: Only upper secondary data refer to the school year 2000. Therefore all others levels have been omitted.

France: Only students administered by the Ministry of Education are included in this chapter, *i.e.* students administered by the Ministry of Health have been omitted. This probably inflates the distribution of students in regular classes.

Germany: Data on students in special classes are included in special schools (for all categories). The distribution of pre-primary to public and private institutions is estimated for all categories.

Greece: Special schools: the available data for lower and upper secondary education are combined. Regular classes: in the Greek educational system these are under special classes.

Italy: In regular classes pre-primary schools dependent of municipalities are not included: there are about 1 700 (estimated) children with disabilities. Figures are estimated for the total number of students in the different phases of education.

Mexico: Upper secondary education does not apply. In special classes totals only are available, there is no individual breakdown of category.

Spain: The numbers of students in special classes are included in special schools. There are a small number of students in special classes, but for the Spanish educational system these classes are considered to be special schools.

Switzerland: Data regarding students in regular classes are missing. Data relating to the Swiss education statistics have been compiled according to classes. Therefore there are no statistical data on aspects of integrated education. Data on students, teachers and financial resources are not derived from a single source. As a consequence it is not possible to combine the various information in a regular manner. Besides, information on financial resources is difficult to obtain on a reliable basis and therefore not provided. Teachers are the only category on which statistical data on staff exist. Nevertheless even such information is limited and not as detailed as the categories of disabilities in students. The entire data on special education are limited to a single description of "compulsory schooling". The different ISCED levels cannot be separated out.

United Kingdom (Eng.): Data include figures collected for England only. Special classes are included in regular classes.

Sweden: Since data are incomplete they are not included in Chapters 3, 4 and 5.

Chapter 4
Analysis of the quantitative data for cross-national categories A, B and C

Background

This analysis follows an identical format to that in the corresponding chapter in the earlier publication *Equity in Education: Students with Disabilities, Learning Difficulties and Disadvantages* (OECD, 2004) which was based on the 1998/99 round of data collection.

As in earlier data collections (see also OECD, 2000b), the amount of information which countries were able to provide varied widely from country to country. There continues to be an overall trend for the most detailed information to be available about provision in special schools, for substantially less information about special classes in regular or mainstream schools, and for there to be very patchy data on students fully integrated in regular classes in regular schools.

The three cross-national categories correspond broadly to students with *disabilities* (A); students with *difficulties* (B); and those with *disadvantages* (C) (see Chapter 1). To avoid extensive repetition of the phrase "students within cross-national category", the terms disabilities, difficulties, and disadvantages are frequently used in this chapter as synonyms for the three cross-national categories. As previously, there are more extensive and reliable data for students with disabilities (relating broadly to what might be called organic defects relating to sensory, motor, or neurological systems) than for those with difficulties or disadvantages.

The chapter is divided into sections covering each of the cross-national categories in turn. Within each section there is an initial discussion of data on students receiving additional resources over the period of compulsory education. This is followed by discussion of data on the various phases of education in turn (*i.e.* pre-primary, primary or basic school education, lower secondary education, and upper secondary education).

Comparisons between the 1998/99 and 2001 data sets are not attempted here. However, comparisons between data sets that illustrate possible trends over time will be a major feature of a forthcoming monograph.

Availability of data

The table in Annex 2 illustrates the availability of data for the cross-national categories for different countries, split according to the location of education (special schools, special classes and regular classes) and its level or phase (compulsory education, pre-primary, primary, lower secondary and upper secondary). As discussed above, considerable gaps in data availability remain, particularly for categories B and C.

Quantitative data on cross-national category A (students receiving additional resources for disabilities)

Cross-national category A, as discussed and defined in Chapter 1, roughly corresponds to needs arising from impairing conditions. All countries using categorical systems for special educational needs have national categories which they consider to fall within cross-national category A, although the number of such categories varies widely from country to country (see Table 2.2 in Chapter 2 for details).

The period of compulsory education

Chart 4.1 shows the number of students receiving additional resources within the period of compulsory education who are considered to fall within cross-national category A for different countries, as a percentage of all students in compulsory education (the period of compulsory education differs from country to country, see Annex 3). Values range from 0.47% (Korea) to 5.16% (USA). The median number of students receiving additional resources for disabilities, for the 17 countries reporting full data, as a percentage of all students in compulsory education is 2.73%, with an inter-quartile range[1] of 1.54% to 3.58%.

Although wide variation continues to exist between countries in terms of students receiving additional resources for disabilities, the differences are substantially less than the differences between countries for some individual categories discussed in the previous chapter. This again confirms the use of an overall disability category as part of the tri-partite approach and increases confidence that like is being compared with like. However, the remaining differences still require explanation. For example, Belgium (Fl.) and the Netherlands might be expected to have similar proportions of students with disabilities; however the proportion for Flanders is approximately twice that of the Netherlands.

The extent to which students receiving additional resources for disabilities are educated within segregated settings also varies widely between countries as shown in Chart 4.2. All students with disabilities are educated in regular mainstream classes in the New Brunswick province of Canada. Over 80% of such students are in special schools in Belgium (Fr.), Czech Republic, Germany and the Netherlands. Over two-thirds of these students are in some form of segregated setting (special school or special class) in 10 of the 14 countries for which the data are available (note that in the United Kingdom [Eng.]

---

1. The statistics reported here (and for other phases of education) are a simplified version of quartiles. The median (Mdn) (or second quartile) is the central data point in an ordered set of data points. The first quartile (Q_1) is taken as the central data point of those points below the median. The third quartile (Q_3) is taken as the central data point of those points above the median. The inter-quartile range is ($Q_3 - Q_1$). For an even number of data points a quartile is taken as the average of the two central points. It is only reported when data are available from at least nine countries.

Examples:

15 data points - $Q_1 = 4^{th}$, Mdn = 8th, $Q_3 = 12^{th}$ point.

10 data points - $Q_1 = 3^{rd}$, Mdn = ave of 5th & 6th, $Q_3 = 8^{h}$ point).

12 data points - $Q_1 = $ ave of 3rd & 4th, Mdn = ave of 6th & 7th, $Q_3 = $ ave of 9^{h} & 10th point.

it is not possible to compute this as students in special classes and regular classes are not counted separately).

Chart 4.1. **Numbers of students receiving additional resources over the period of compulsory education in cross-national category A, as a percentage of all students in compulsory education, 2001**[1]

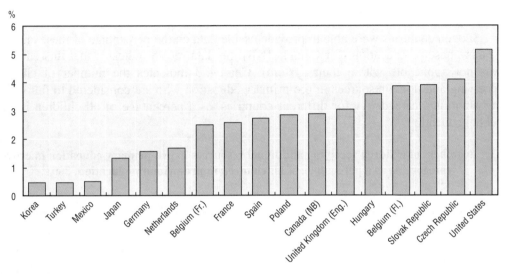

1. France: for the sake of international comparability French students administered by the Ministry of Health have been added to these data provided by the Ministry of Education. This probably has the effect of slightly inflating the percentage for France in contrast to other countries that have an unknown number of students outside the education system.

Chart 4.2. **Percentage of students receiving additional resources over the period of compulsory education in cross-national category A by location**[1,2,3,4]

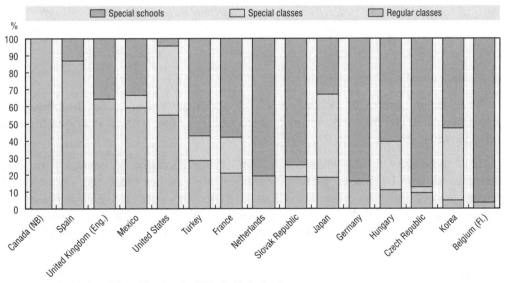

1. Special classes: not applicable in Belgium (Fl.), Canada (NB), the Netherlands.
2. Special classes: included in special schools in Germany and Spain.
3. Special classes: included in regular classes in England.
4. Special schools: not applicable in Canada (NB).

Pre-primary education

Pre-primary education (*i.e.* that which is provided before the normal age at which children are required to attend school) is regarded by many as an important service for children with special educational needs. By providing early intervention for those who are likely to have difficulties in accessing the school curriculum, it may well be that such later problems are reduced.

Sixteen countries were able to provide usable data on the percentage of these children in this phase of education (for Canada [NB] the data return indicates that this category was not applicable within their system). Chart 4.3 indicates the number of children receiving additional resources in pre-primary education who are considered to fall within cross-national category A for different countries, as a percentage of all children in pre-school education.

Chart 4.3.   **Numbers of children receiving additional resources in pre-primary education in cross-national category A, as a percentage of all children in pre-primary education, 2001[1]**

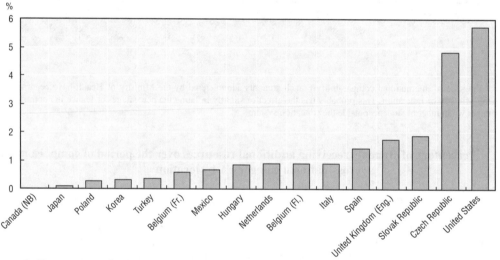

1. Countries are ranked in ascending order of percentage of students.

The median number of students receiving additional resources for disabilities as a percentage of all children in pre-primary education is 0.86%, with an inter-quartile range of 0.35% to 1.51%.

It is noteworthy that, as shown in Table 4.1, for 15 of the 16 countries for which comparisons can be made, these percentages are smaller than the corresponding percentages at primary level (see also Chart 4.5). Median values are 0.86% at pre-primary and 2.54% at primary level; this difference reaches statistical significance – Wilcoxon test n = 16, T = 3 p<0.05. However, the interpretation of this result requires further analytic work.

Chart 4.4 shows that pre-primary children with disabilities are in segregated special centres in Japan and in the Netherlands. In five of the twelve countries for which data are available, three-quarters or more of pre-primary children with disabilities attend segregated special centres or special classes (note that in the United Kingdom [Eng.] it is not possible to compute this as students in special classes and regular classes are not counted separately). In Spain and Italy, however, nearly all such children are integrated into regular provision (87% and 99% respectively).

Table 4.1.   **Comparison of numbers of children with disabilities receiving additional resources in pre-primary and primary education, as a percentage of all children in that phase of education**

	Pre-primary	Primary
Canada (NB)	0.00	2.19
Japan	0.09	1.42
Poland	0.29	2.66
Korea	0.30	0.46
Turkey	0.37	0.49
Belgium (Fr.)	0.57	2.01
Mexico	0.68	0.91
Hungary	0.85	4.18
Italy	0.88	2.03
Belgium (Fl.)	0.88	3.61
Netherlands	0.93	2.70
Spain	1.43	3.33
United Kingdom (Eng.)	1.75	2.43
Slovak Republic	1.86	4.37
Czech Republic	4.83	4.17
United States	5.75	6.08

Chart 4.4.   **Percentages of children receiving additional resources in pre-primary education in cross-national category A by location[1, 2, 3, 4]**

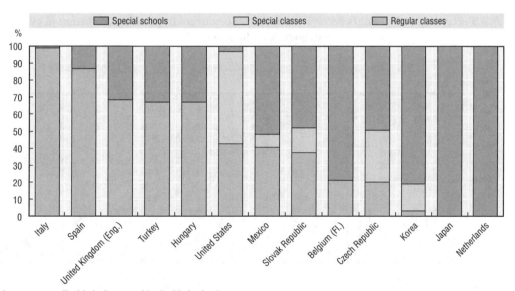

1. Regular classes: not applicable in Japan and in the Netherlands.
2. Special classes: not applicable in Belgium (Fl.), in Japan, in the Netherlands and in Turkey.
3. Special classes: included in special schools in Spain.
4. Special classes: included in regular classes in England.

Primary education

As indicated above there are typically higher percentages of students with disabilities receiving additional resources at primary level than at pre-primary. Chart 4.5 provides details. The overall median value for the 16 countries providing usable data is 2.54%, with an inter-quartile range of 1.87% to 3.75%, with the United States (6.08%) as the only outstanding outlier.

Chart 4.5.   **Numbers of students receiving additional resources in primary education in cross-national category A, as a percentage of all children in primary education, 2001[1]**

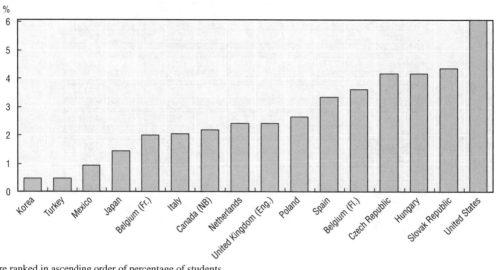

1. Countries are ranked in ascending order of percentage of students.

Chart 4.6.   **Percentages of students receiving additional resources in primary education in cross-national category A by location[1, 2, 3, 4]**

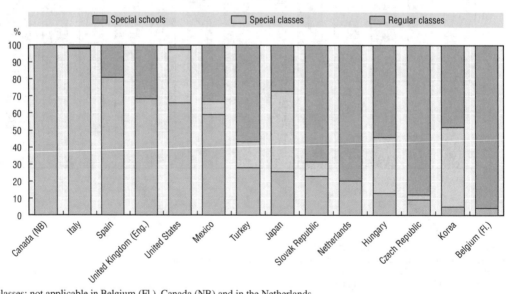

1. Special classes: not applicable in Belgium (Fl.), Canada (NB) and in the Netherlands.
2. Special classes: included in special schools in Spain.
3. Special classes: included in regular classes in the United Kingdom (Eng.).
4. Special schools: not applicable in Canada (NB).

The location of the education of cross-national category A students at primary level is shown in Chart 4.6. The picture is again of the full range between large-scale integration in the regular classes of mainstream schools (Canada [NB] 100%, Italy 98%) and virtually total (96%) segregation in special schools in Belgium (Fl.). This divergence is further illustrated by the fact that six of the fourteen countries represented have a majority of these students receiving additional resources for disabilities in segregated special schools, while five of them have a majority of these students in fully integrated regular classes (the United Kingdom [Eng.] presents aggregate figures where students in special classes are included in regular classes, hence the percentage in regular classes cannot be determined). One third or more of these students in Hungary, Japan and Korea are in special classes.

Lower secondary education

Chart 4.7 shows the number of students with disabilities receiving additional resources in lower secondary education (again as a percentage of all students at that level). The overall median value for the 15 countries providing full data is 3.56% with an inter-quartile range of 2.00% to 4.71%. This shows somewhat greater variability than was found at primary level, also with more extreme outliers, 0.24% in Mexico to 8.59% in Belgium (Fr.).

However there is no consistent pattern for the relative size of percentages in the two phases of education, as shown in Table 4.2. The median value at primary level for the 14 countries for which there are data at lower secondary is slightly lower (2.68% for primary and 3.68% for lower secondary), but seven countries show a decreased percentage at lower secondary compared with primary while the other half of the countries show an increased percentage.

Chart 4.7. **Numbers of students receiving additional resources in lower secondary education in cross-national category A, as a percentage of all students in lower secondary education, 2001[1]**

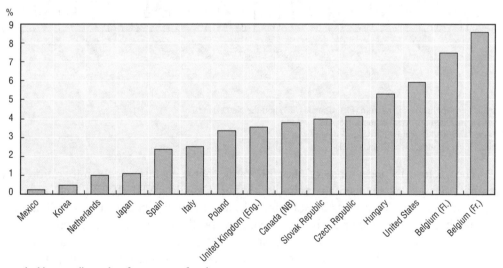

1. Countries are ranked in ascending order of percentage of students.

Data on the location of the education of students with disabilities receiving additional resources shows a very similar pattern at lower secondary to that at primary level and is displayed in Chart 4.8.

Table 4.2. **Comparison of numbers of children with disabilities receiving additional resources in primary and lower secondary education, as a percentage of all children in that phase of education**

	Primary	Lower secondary
Mexico	0.91	0.24
Japan	1.42	1.09
Belgium (Fr.)	2.01	8.59
Italy	2.03	2.53
Canada (NB)	2.19	3.80
United Kingdom (Eng.)	2.43	3.56
Poland	2.66	3.38
Netherlands	2.70	1.61
Spain	3.33	2.39
Belgium (Fl.)	3.61	7.51
Czech Republic	4.17	4.13
Hungary	4.18	5.29
Slovak Republic	4.37	3.96
United States	6.08	5.92

Chart 4.8. **Percentages of students receiving additional resources in lower secondary education in cross-national category A by location**[1, 2, 3, 4]

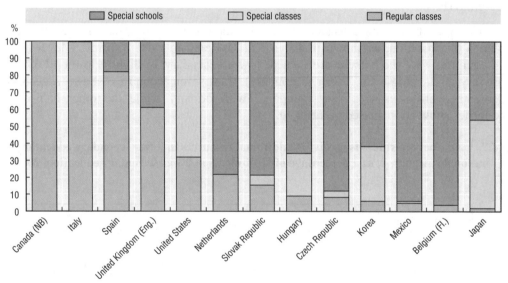

1. Special classes: not applicable in Belgium (Fl.), Canada (NB) and the Netherlands.
2. Special classes: included in special schools in Spain.
3. Special classes: included in regular classes in England.
4. Special schools: not applicable for Canada (NB).

The picture is once more of the full range between large-scale integration in the regular classes of mainstream schools (again Canada [NB] 100%) and over 90% segregation in special schools in Belgium (Fl.) and Mexico. There is also a similar pattern in that half of the countries have a majority of these students receiving additional resources for disabilities in segregated special schools, while three have a majority of these students in fully integrated regular classes (the United Kingdom [Eng.] again presents aggregate figures where students in special classes are included in regular classes, hence the percentage in regular classes cannot be determined).

Generally countries with largely integrated or largely segregated provision maintain the same pattern of provision at lower secondary as at primary level, Mexico is an exception, while there was a majority (59%) of students with disabilities in regular classes at primary level, this reduces to 5% at lower secondary level, with 94% being educated in segregated special schools at lower secondary level.

Upper secondary education

Chart 4.9 shows the number of students with disabilities receiving additional resources in upper secondary education (again as a percentage of all students at that level). The overall median value for the 14 countries providing usable data is 1.22% with an inter-quartile range of 0.89% to 2.44%. Five of the fourteen show values less than 1%. The United Kingdom (Eng.) provides an upper value outlier at 4.19% which, given that it also had a similar extreme high value at pre-primary level, suggests a concern for extending the age range of educational provision where additional resources are provided for students with disabilities.

Chart 4.9. **Numbers of students receiving additional resources in upper secondary education in cross-national category A, as a percentage of all students in upper secondary education, 2001[1]**

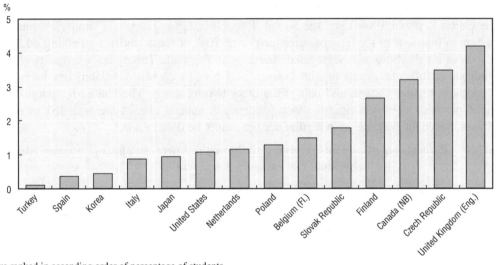

1. Countries are ranked in ascending order of percentage of students.

There is a strong tendency for the relative size of percentages in upper secondary to be smaller than those at lower secondary, as shown in Table 4.3. The median value at upper secondary level for the 12 countries for which there are data at lower secondary is lower (1.22% as against 3.47%), this difference reaching statistical significance – Wilcoxon test n= 12, T = 3 p<0.05. Eleven of the countries show a decreased percentage at upper secondary compared with lower. Only one country, the United Kingdom (Eng.), shows an increased percentage, reinforcing the view stated above that they have a concern for extending the age range of educational provision for students with disabilities.

Table 4.3. **Comparison of numbers of children with disabilities receiving additional resources in lower and upper secondary education, as a percentage of all children in that phase of education**

	Lower secondary	Upper secondary
Korea	0.49	0.44
Japan	1.09	0.94
Netherlands	1.61	1.16
Spain	2.39	0.36
Italy	2.53	0.87
Poland	3.38	1.28
United Kingdom (Eng.)	3.56	4.19
Canada (NB)	3.80	3.21
Slovak Republic	3.96	1.78
Czech Republic	4.13	3.48
United States	5.92	1.07
Belgium (Fl)	7.51	1.48

Data on the location of the education of students with disabilities receiving additional resources show a very similar pattern at upper secondary to that at primary and lower secondary level and are displayed in Chart 4.10. The picture is again of the full range between large-scale integration in the regular classes of mainstream schools (Canada [NB] and Spain 100%; Italy 99%) and total or virtually total segregation in special schools in Japan (100%), the Czech Republic (96%) and the Slovak Republic (92%). There is a similarly contrasting pattern in that four of the ten countries have over 70% of these students receiving additional resources for disabilities in segregated special schools, while Turkey has a majority of these students in fully integrated regular classes, and a sixth country (Finland) has half of the students in regular classes, and half in the other two locations. The United Kingdom (Eng.) again presents aggregate figures where students in special classes are included in regular classes, hence the percentage in regular classes cannot be determined.

Chart 4.10. **Percentages of students receiving additional resources in upper secondary education in cross-national category A by location[1, 2, 3, 4, 5]**

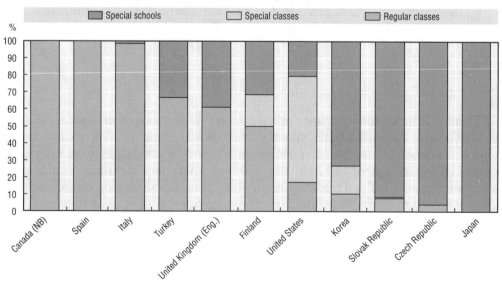

1. Regular classes: not applicable in Japan.
2. Special classes: not applicable in Canada (NB), Turkey.
3. Special classes: included in special schools in Spain.
4. Special classes: included in regular classes in the United Kingdom (Eng.).
5. Special schools: not applicable in Canada (NB).

In most cases countries with largely integrated or largely segregated provision at lower secondary level maintain the same pattern of provision at upper secondary.

Quantitative data on cross-national category B (students receiving additional resources for difficulties)

As previously discussed the quantity and quality of data relating to cross-national categories B and C are inferior to that for cross-national category A. Cross-national category B, as discussed and defined in Chapter 1, refers to students with behavioural or emotional disorders, or specific difficulties in learning. The educational need is considered to arise primarily from problems in the interaction between the student and the educational context.

While all countries using categorical systems for special educational needs have national categories which they consider to fall within cross-national category A, two countries (Italy and Japan) placed no categories in cross-national category B. In Turkey the only such category is that of "gifted and talented" which is considered separately from other categories as discussed in Chapter 3 (see Table 2.2 in Chapter 2 for details) and is not included in these analyses.

The period of compulsory education

Chart 4.11 shows the number of students receiving additional resources within the period of compulsory education who are considered to fall within cross-national category B for different countries, as a percentage of all students in compulsory education. Those countries which have no national categories falling within cross-national category B (*i.e.* for whom a zero is entered because the category is not applicable) are included in the chart as this implies that there are no cross-national category B students receiving additional resources. Including these, 17 countries provide full data. The median number of category B students as a percentage of all students in compulsory education is 2.15%. The inter-quartile range from 0.71% to 5.51% indicates an amount of variability far in excess of that found in the corresponding data for students with disabilities (1.54% to 3.58%).

Limiting the analysis to those countries with national categories falling within cross-national category B, data are available from 15 countries (median percentage 2.18%; inter-quartile range from 1.31% to 6.01%). Taking these figures together with the high values of 17.70% (United Kingdom [Eng.]) and 22.29% (Poland) which greatly exceed corresponding percentages for students with disabilities (3.03% and 2.85% respectively), it appears that when such categories are recognised in national systems the numbers of students receiving additional resources are considerable.

Chart 4.12 presents data from 15 countries on the location of students receiving additional resources for learning and other difficulties. While again showing major country-to-country variation, the typical pattern is for at least two thirds of such students to be educated in regular classes in mainstream schools. This is true for half of the countries where the data enable this to be decided (in the United Kingdom [Eng.] while fewer than 1% are educated in special schools, it is not known how the remaining students are divided between special classes and regular classes).

Important exceptions are Belgium (Fr.) (100%) and Belgium (Fl.) (98%) where almost all such students are educated in special schools, France where 69% are in special schools (and the rest in special classes), and the Netherlands where only 2% of students receiving additional resources because of learning and other difficulties are educated in regular classes, the rest being mainly in special classes (61%). In Germany 12% are in regular classes, but the split of the remainder between special classes and special schools is not available. Apart from the Netherlands, two other countries, Korea (62%) and the United States (55%), place most of these students in special classes.

Chart 4.11. **Numbers of students receiving additional resources over the period of compulsory education in cross-national category B, as a percentage of all students in compulsory education, 2001[1, 2]**

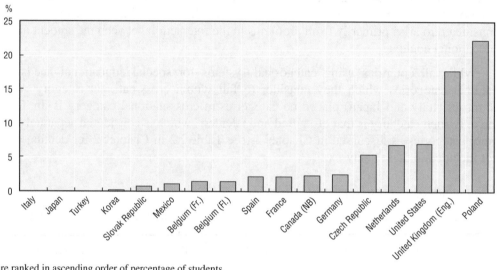

1. Countries are ranked in ascending order of percentage of students.
2. In Italy and Japan there are no national categories falling within category B.

Chart 4.12. **Percentages of students receiving additional resources over the period of compulsory education in cross-national category B by location[1, 2, 3]**

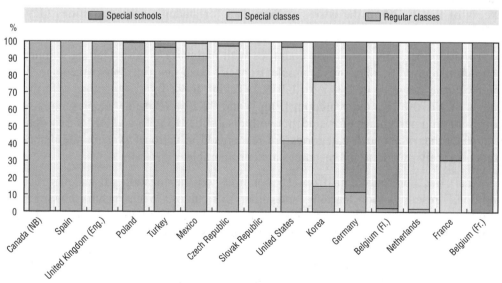

1. Regular classes: not applicable in Belgium (Fr.) and France.
2. Special classes: not applicable in Belgium (Fl.), Belgium (Fr.), Canada (NB), and Spain; included in special schools in Germany.
3. Special schools: not applicable in Canada (NB) and Spain.

Pre-primary education

Chart 4.13 indicates the number of children receiving additional resources in pre-school education who are considered to fall within cross-national category B for different countries, as a percentage of all children in pre-school education. While 16 countries are included in the chart, five of them provide zero values, either because the category is not applicable (*e.g.* no B categories in the national system), or is a known zero figure. The median value for the number of children receiving additional resources because of difficulties is 0.07%, with an inter-quartile range of 0% to 0.29%.

Chart 4.13. **Numbers of children receiving resources in pre-primary education in cross-national category B, as a percentage of all children in pre-primary education, 2001**[1, 2, 3]

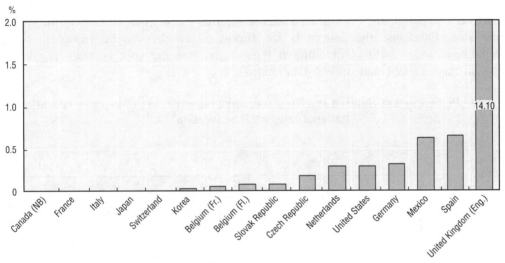

1. Countries are ranked in ascending order of percentage of students.
2. In Italy and Japan there are no national categories falling within category B.
3. Although there are national categories falling within category B in France no children are in this category in pre-primary education.

However, while it appears that typically countries provide little or no additional resources at pre-school level for these children, the United Kingdom (Eng.) (14.10%) provides a notable exception.

Table 4.4. **Comparison of numbers of children with difficulties receiving additional resources in pre-primary and primary education, as a percentage of all children in that phase of education**

	Pre-primary	Primary
France	0.00	0.46
Canada (New Brunswick)	0.00	2.19
Korea	0.03	0.31
Belgium (Fr.)	0.05	2.30
Belgium (Fl.)	0.07	2.66
Slovak Republic	0.07	0.78
Czech Republic	0.17	5.14
Netherlands	0.28	4.06
United States	0.29	4.89
Mexico	0.61	1.83
Spain	0.65	2.04
United Kingdom (Eng.)	14.10	19.44

As was found above in analysing the data on children with disabilities, these percentages are smaller than the corresponding percentages at primary level (see also Chart 4.15). Table 4.4 gives details for the 12 countries where comparisons can be made (excluding countries with no B categories). For all 12 countries percentages are greater at primary level giving a statistically significant result (Wilcoxon test n = 12 T = 0 p<0.05).

Median values for this restricted set are 0.12% at pre-primary and 2.24% at primary level. This difference is perhaps not surprising since the identification of category B students is dependent on them having attended school.

Chart 4.14 shows that only ten countries can provide full data on the location of pre-school education for children with difficulties. In Belgium (Fr.) and Germany all such children are placed in special centres and in Belgium (Fl.) this is the case for 99% of them. In Korea all but 5% are placed either in special centres or special classes, while in the Czech Republic and the United States substantial use is made of each of the types of provision. Otherwise the pattern is for almost all children to be placed in regular integrated classes with other children (note again that the split between regular and special classes is not made in UK data returns).

Chart 4.14. **Percentages of children receiving additional resources in pre-primary education in cross-national category B by location**[1, 2, 3, 4]

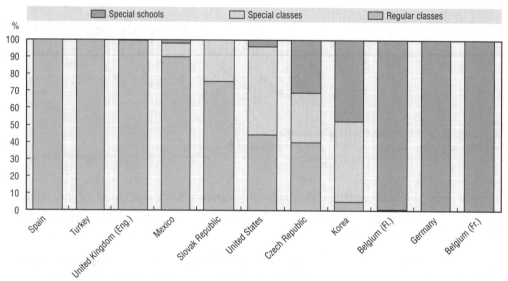

1. Regular classes: not applicable in Belgium (Fr.).
2. Special classes: not applicable in Belgium (Fl.), Belgium (Fr.) and Spain.
3. Special classes: included in special centres in Germany.
4. Special classes: included in regular classes in the United Kingdom (Eng.).

Primary education

Chart 4.15 provides details of the number of students with difficulties receiving additional resources at primary level as a percentage of all students in primary education. The overall median value for the 14 countries providing full data (including 2 for which zeroes are entered) is 2.08%, with an inter-quartile range of 0.54% to 3.71%. A notable feature is that the United Kingdom (Eng.) (19.44%) approaches 20%.

Chart 4.15. **Numbers of students receiving additional resources in primary education in cross-national category B, as a percentage of all students in primary education, 2001[1, 2]**

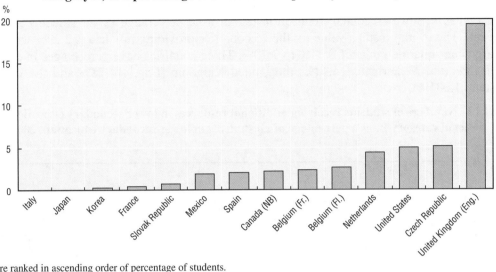

1. Countries are ranked in ascending order of percentage of students.
2. In Italy and Japan there are no national categories falling within category B.

Twelve countries provided full data on the location of the education of cross-national category B students at primary level, as shown in Chart 4.16. In about half of the countries 80% or more of these students are educated in regular classrooms. The main exceptions are Belgium (Fr.) and the Netherlands, where they are all in special schools, Belgium (Fl.) where the vast majority of these students are in special schools, France where they are either in special schools (35%) or special classes (65%), and Korea, where almost all (89%) are in special classes. As at other phases of education in the United Kingdom (Eng.) while fewer than 1% are educated in special schools, it is not known how the rest are divided between special classes and regular classes.

Chart 4.16. **Percentages of students receiving additional resources in primary education in cross-national category B by location[1, 2, 3, 4]**

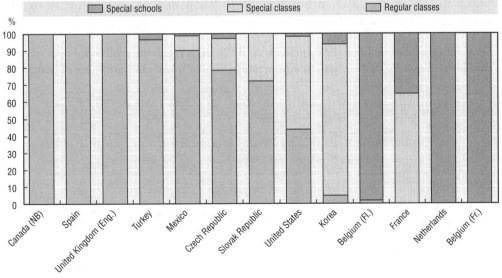

1. Regular classes: not applicable in Belgium (Fr.) and France.
2. Special classes: not applicable in Belgium (Fl.), Belgium (Fr.), Canada (NB), the Netherlands and Spain.
3. Special classes: included in regular classes in the United Kingdom (Eng.).
4. Special schools: not applicable in Canada (NB).

Lower secondary education

Chart 4.17 shows the number of students with difficulties receiving additional resources in lower secondary education (again as a percentage of all students at that level). The overall median value for the 15 countries providing full data is 2.29% with the large inter-quartile range of 0.34% to 7.70%. Three countries have percentages in excess of 10% (the Netherlands 14.44%, the United Kingdom [Eng.] 14.78% and the United States 15.31%).

Chart 4.17. **Numbers of students receiving additional resources in lower secondary education in cross-national category B, as a percentage of all students in lower secondary education, 2001[1, 2]**

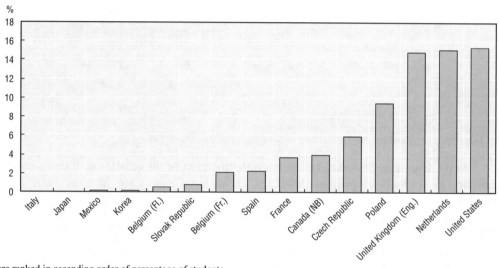

1. Countries are ranked in ascending order of percentage of students.
2. In Italy and Japan there are no national categories falling within category B.

If the analysis is restricted to those countries presenting data at both primary and lower secondary levels (excluding countries with no categories in cross-national category B), there is no pattern for students with difficulties for an increase or a decrease (6 decrease and 6 increase) in the percentage when moving from primary to lower secondary, as illustrated in Table 4.5.

Table 4.5. **Comparison of numbers of students with difficulties receiving additional resources in primary and lower secondary education, as a percentage of all students in that phase of education**

	Primary	Lower secondary
Korea	0.31	0.12
France	0.46	3.71
Slovak Republic	0.78	0.75
Mexico	1.83	0.07
Spain	2.04	2.29
Canada (NB)	2.12	3.90
Belgium (Fr.)	2.30	2.07
Belgium (Fl.)	2.66	0.56
Netherlands	4.06	14.44
United States	4.89	15.31
Czech Republic	5.14	5.93
United Kingdom (Eng.)	19.44	14.78

However, the median primary percentage (2.21%) is somewhat lower than that at lower secondary (3.00%), a difference which does not approach statistical significance (Wilcoxon test n = 12 T = 38 p>0.05).

Data on the location of the education of students with difficulties receiving additional resources are shown in Chart 4.18. Most countries show a very similar pattern at lower secondary to that at primary level. However, the Netherlands and France show major changes. In the Netherlands the change is from exclusive use of special schools to 97% in special classes at lower secondary. And in France the 35/65 split in the relative use of special schools and special classes at primary level is exactly reversed at lower secondary.

Chart 4.18. **Percentage of students receiving additional resources in lower secondary education in cross-national category B by location**[1, 2, 3, 4]

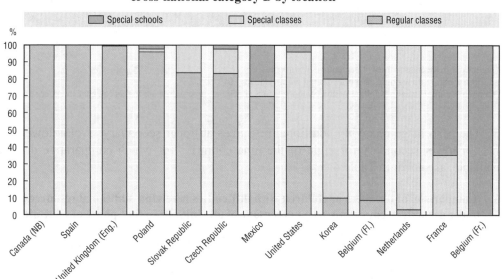

1. Regular classes: not applicable in Belgium (Fr.) and France.
2. Special classes: not applicable in Belgium (Fl.), Belgium (Fr.), Canada (NB) and Spain.
3. Special classes: included in regular classes in United Kingdom (Eng.).
4. Special schools: not applicable in Canada (NB).

Upper secondary education

Chart 4.19 shows the number of students with difficulties receiving additional resources in upper secondary education (again as a percentage of all students at that level). In half of the countries for which full data are available the percentage receiving additional resources at this level of education is very small (0.03% or fewer). The median value is 0.03% with an inter-quartile range of 0% to 1.55%.

Chart 4.19. **Numbers of students receiving additional resources in upper secondary education in cross-national category B, as a percentage of all students in upper secondary education, 2001[1, 2, 3]**

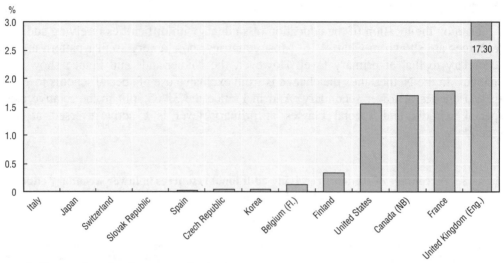

1. Countries are ranked in ascending order of percentage of students.
2. In Italy and Japan there are no national categories falling within category B.
3. Although there are national categories falling within category B in Switzerland, no children are in this category in upper secondary education.

The percentage receiving additional resources at upper secondary level is lower than that for lower secondary for eight of the nine countries for which comparative data are available, as shown in Table 4.6.

Table 4.6. **Comparison of numbers of children with difficulties receiving additional resources in lower and upper secondary education, as a percentage of all children in that phase of education**

	Lower secondary	Upper secondary
Korea	0.12	0.03
Belgium (Fl)	0.56	0.12
Slovak Republic	0.75	0.00
Spain	2.29	0.01
France	3.71	1.79
Canada (NB)	3.90	1.70
Czech Republic	5.93	0.03
United Kingdom (Eng.)	14.78	17.30
United States	15.31	1.55

The exception is the United Kingdom (Eng.) which shows an increase from 14.78% to 17.30%. The median percentage drops from 3.71% at lower secondary to 0.12% at upper secondary (the difference is statistically significant (Wilcoxon test, N = 9 T = 3 p<0.05).

Adequate data on the location of the education of these students at upper secondary level are available for seven countries as shown in Chart 4.20. The patterns are similar to those at lower secondary. Korea, Finland and the United States are the three countries for which data are available making use of segregated provision at this level, with the proportion of students in special schools or classes increasing from lower to upper secondary in Korea. As at other levels of education the United Kingdom (Eng.) data do not permit separate assessment of the numbers of students in special or regular classes.

Chart 4.20. **Percentages of students receiving additional resources in upper secondary education in cross-national category B by location[1, 2, 3]**

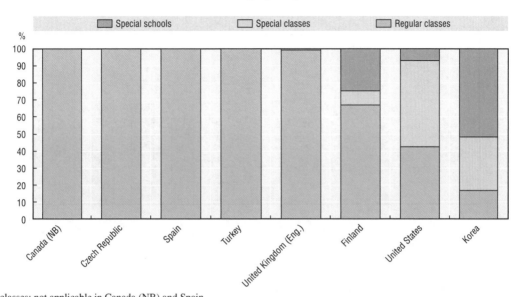

1. Special classes: not applicable in Canada (NB) and Spain.
2. Special classes: included in regular classes in the United Kingdom (Eng.).
3. Special schools: not applicable in Canada (NB).

Quantitative data on cross-national category C (students receiving additional resources for disadvantages)

Cross-national category C, as discussed and defined in Chapter 1, covers those national categories referring to students considered to have special needs arising from disadvantages in their socio-economic background. Three countries (Germany, Korea and the United Kingdom [Eng.]) had no categories which they placed in cross-national category C (see Table 2.2).

The period of compulsory education

Chart 4.21 shows the number of students receiving additional resources within the period of compulsory education who are considered to fall within cross-national category C for different countries, as a percentage of all students in compulsory education (the period of compulsory education differs from country to country – see Annex 3). Those countries who have no national categories falling within cross-national category C (*i.e.* for whom a zero is entered because the category is not applicable) are, as with cross-national category B charts, included in the chart as this implies that there are no cross-national category C students receiving additional resources. Including these, 12 countries provided data, the median number of category C students as a percentage of all students in compulsory education being 2.88%. The large inter-quartile range is from 0.00% to 14.96%.

Chart 4.21. **Numbers of students receiving additional resources over the period of compulsory education in cross-national category C, as a percentage of all students in compulsory education**[1, 2, 3, 4]

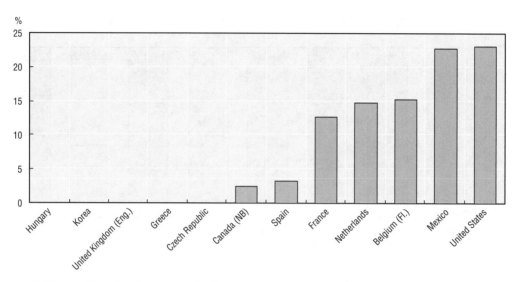

1. Countries are ranked in ascending order of percentage of students.
2. In Korea and the United Kingdom (Eng.) there are no national categories falling within category C.
3. Greece: category 8 "socio-economic/cultural educational difficulties" is not available in regular classes.
4. Hungary: category 9 "disadvantaged students" is not available.

This median percentage for C (2.88%) is slightly greater than that for A (2.73%) and far greater than for B (2.15%). The central range (0.00% to 14.96%) is substantially larger than that for A (1.54% to 3.58%), but more similar to that for B (0.71% to 5.51%). Table 4.7 provides comparison data restricted to those countries for which data are available for all cross-national categories. The median values for A, B and C respectively are now 2.73%, 2.38% and 3.30%. Inter-quartile ranges are 1.81% to 3.65% for A, 1.84% to 4.79% for B, and 0.04% to 14.61% for C. The ranges increase substantially from A to B, and from B to C (illustrating how comparisons where different countries enter into the comparisons are potentially misleading).

Table 4.7. **Comparison of percentages of children in cross-national categories A, B and C over the period of compulsory education (countries for which data are available for all three categories)**

	A	B	C
Netherlands	2.08	6.52	14.85
Spain	2.73	2.15	3.30
Belgium (Fl.)	3.86	1.53	15.29
Canada (NB)	2.89	2.38	2.46
United States	5.16	7.13	23.07
Korea	0.47	0.09	0.00
Mexico	0.51	1.13	22.74
Germany	1.54	2.61	0.00
France	2.58	2.18	12.59
United Kingdom	3.03	17.70	0.00
Czech Republic	4.08	5.51	0.08

Limiting the cross-national category C analysis to those countries with national categories falling within C, data are available from 10 countries (median percentage 7.94%; quartiles 0.67% and 15.18%). Taking these figures together with the high values of 12.59% (France), 14.85% (Netherlands), 15.29% (Belgium [Fl.]), 23.07% (United States) and 22.74% (Mexico) which are very similar to corresponding percentages for students with difficulties – and in both cases of difficulties and disadvantages substantially in excess of the highest percentages reported for students with disabilities – it appears that *when such categories are recognised in national systems* the numbers of students receiving additional resources are considerable.

Chart 4.22. **Percentages of students receiving additional resources in compulsory education in cross-national category C by location[1, 2]**

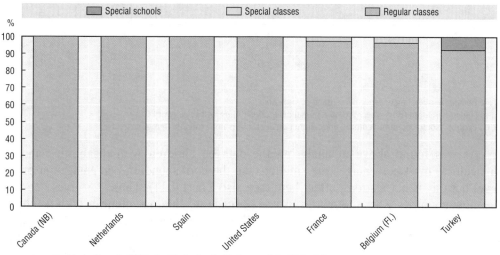

1. Special classes: not applicable in Canada (NB), the Netherlands, Turkey and the United States.
2. Special schools: not applicable in Belgium (Fl.), Canada (NB), Spain, tbe Netherlands, Turkey and the United States.

This conclusion has to be treated with caution since other countries may recognise the need for these students but include funding in regular per capita calculations. Further analytical work is needed.

Chart 4.22 presents data from seven countries on the location of students receiving additional resources for disadvantages. In four of the seven this education is exclusively in regular mainstream classrooms, while in all countries over 90% are in such locations.

Pre-primary education

Chart 4.23 indicates the number of children receiving additional resources in pre-primary education who are considered to fall within cross-national category C for different countries, as a percentage of all children in pre-school education. The median value for the number of children receiving additional resources because of disadvantages is 0.49%, with an inter-quartile range of 0.00% to 3.46%.

While it appears that typically countries provide little or no additional resources at pre-primary level for these children, France (12.99%), the Netherlands (19.24%) and Belgium (Fl.) (25.17%) are notable exceptions.

Chart 4.23. **Numbers of children receiving additional resources in pre-primary education in cross-national category C, as a percentage of all children in pre-primary education, 2001[1, 2, 3]**

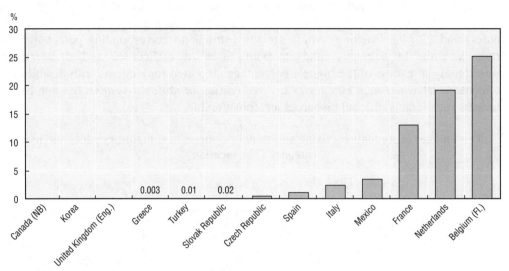

1. Countries are ranked in ascending order of percentage of students.
2. In Korea and United Kingdom (Eng.) there are no national categories falling within category C.
3. In Greece, category 8 "socio-economic/cultural educational difficulties" is not available in regular classes.

As was found above in analysing the data on children with disabilities and with difficulties, most percentages are smaller than the corresponding percentages at primary level but this is not a strong effect here (see also Chart 4.24). Table 4.8 gives details for the eight countries where comparisons can be made (excluding countries with no children in C categories at either level). Median values for this restricted set are 2.22% at pre-primary and 6.81% at primary level, with the primary percentage exceeding that at pre-primary for six of the eight countries for which there is a difference (not statistically significant – Wilcoxon test n = 9 T = 12 p>0.05).

Table 4.8. **Comparison of numbers of children with disadvantages receiving additional resources in pre-primary and primary education, as a percentage of all children in that phase of education**

	Pre-primary	Primary
Greece	0.00	0.01
Slovak Republic	0.02	0.06
Czech Republic	0.49	0.04
Spain	0.99	4.56
Mexico	3.46	34.45
France	12.99	12.74
Netherlands	19.24	21.06
Belgium (Fl.)	25.17	25.44

Seven countries can provide data on the location of pre-primary education for children with difficulties, as shown in Chart 4.24. The Slovak Republic is the only country reporting segregated provision, with all children in special centres. Otherwise the pattern is for all children to be placed in regular integrated classes with other children.

Chart 4.24. **Percentages of students receiving additional resources in pre-primary education in cross-national category C by location[1, 2]**

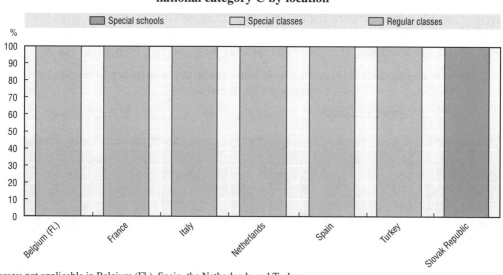

1. Special classes: not applicable in Belgium (Fl.), Spain, the Netherlands and Turkey.
2. Special schools: not applicable in Belgium (Fl.), Spain, France, Italy, the Netherlands and Turkey.

Primary education

Chart 4.25 provides details of the number of students with disadvantages receiving additional resources at primary level as a percentage of all students in primary education. The overall median value for the 17 countries providing data (including three for which zeroes are entered) is 0.121%, with an inter-quartile range of 0.00% to 12.74%. As in the corresponding analysis for students with difficulties at primary level, several countries show high percentages with four exceeding 20% (Netherlands 21.06%, Belgium (Fl.) 25.44%, United States 32.40% and Mexico 34.45%). Note however that these are different countries from those with high percentages for students with difficulties (see Chart 4.15).

Chart 4.25. **Numbers of students receiving additional resources in primary education in cross-national category C, as a percentage of all students in primary education[1, 2, 3, 4]**

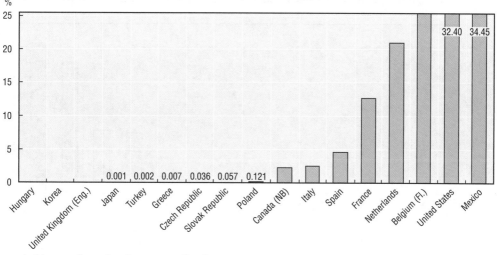

1. Countries are ranked in ascending order of percentage of students.
2. In Korea and the United Kingdom (Eng.) there are no national categories falling within category C.
3. In Greece, category 8 "socio-economic/cultural educational difficulties" is not available in regular classes.
4. In Hungary, category 9 "disadvantaged students" is not available.

The location for the education of these students at primary level shows a similar pattern to that found in pre-primary education, as illustrated in Chart 4.26. Nine countries provide data – five placing all such students in regular integrated classes. The exception is again the Slovak Republic where the provision for socially disadvantaged students is in special schools. There is also some, limited, use of segregated provision in Belgium (Fl.), France and Turkey.

Chart 4.26. **Percentages of students receiving additional resources in primary education in cross-national category C by location[1, 2]**

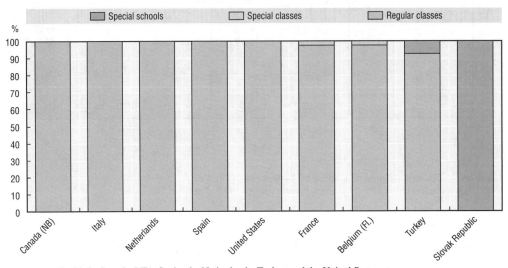

1. Special classes: not applicable in Canada (NB), Spain, the Netherlands, Turkey and the United States.
2. Special schools: not applicable in Belgium (Fl.), Canada (NB), France, Italy, the Netherlands and the United States.

Lower secondary education

Chart 4.27 shows the number of students with disadvantages receiving additional resources in lower secondary education (again as a percentage of all students at that level). The overall median value for the 15 countries providing data is 1.65% with an inter-quartile range of 0.06% to 6.63%.

Chart 4.27. **Numbers of students receiving additional resources in lower secondary education in cross-national category C, as a percentage of all students in lower secondary education, 2001[1, 2, 3]**

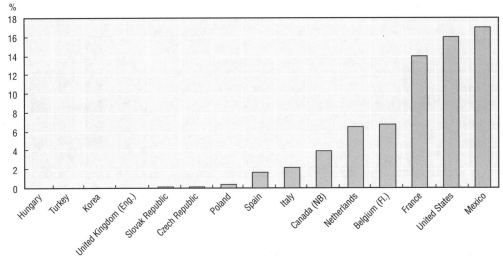

1. Countries are ranked in ascending order of percentage of students.
2. In Korea and the United Kingdom (Eng.) there are no national categories falling within category C.
3. Hungary: category 9 "disadvantaged students" is not available.

If the analysis is restricted to those countries presenting data at both primary and lower secondary levels (excluding countries with no students in cross-national category C at either level), the pattern for students with disadvantages is as illustrated in Table 4.9 (median at primary 4.56%, at lower secondary 3.94%, not statistically significant – Wilcoxon test n = 11 T = 19 p>0.05).

Table 4.9. **Comparison of numbers of children with disadvantages receiving additional resources in primary and lower secondary education, as a percentage of all children in that phase of education**

	Primary	Lower secondary
Czech Republic	0.04	0.15
Slovak Republic	0.06	0.13
Poland	0.12	0.34
Canada (NB)	2.18	3.94
Italy	2.49	2.14
Spain	4.56	1.65
France	12.74	13.88
Netherlands	21.06	6.49
Belgium (Fl.)	25.44	6.77
United States	32.40	16.02
Mexico	34.45	16.98

Data on the location of the education of students with disadvantages receiving additional resources are essentially identical to that at primary level, as shown in Chart 4.28.

Chart 4.28. **Percentages of students receiving additional resources in lower secondary education in cross-national category C by location[1, 2]**

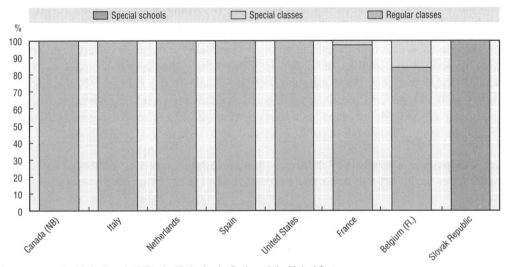

1. Special classes: not applicable in Canada (NB), the Netherlands, Spain and the United States.
2. Special schools: not applicable in Belgium (Fl.), Canada (NB), France, Italy, the Netherlands and the United States.

Upper secondary education

Chart 4.29 shows the number of students with disadvantages receiving additional resources in upper secondary education (again as a percentage of all students at that level). Of the 16 countries for which data are available there are no additional resources for students with disadvantages in six countries. The overall median percentage is 0.07%, with an inter-quartile range of 0.00% to 1.30%. The French community in Belgium provides an extreme outlier (26.95%), almost eight times greater than the next highest percentage.

Chart 4.29. Numbers of students receiving additional resources in upper secondary in cross-national category C, as a percentage of all students in upper secondary education, 2001[1, 2, 3, 4]

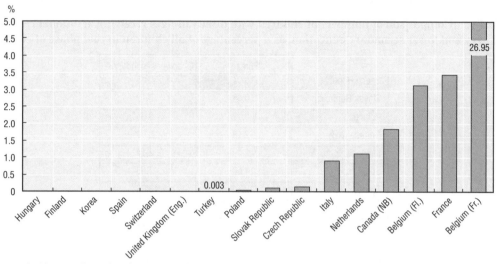

1. Countries are ranked in ascending order of percentage of students.
2. In Korea and the United Kingdom (Eng.) there are no national categories falling within category C.
3. Although there are national categories falling within category C in Finland, Spain and Switzerland, no children are in this category in upper secondary education.
4. In Hungary, category 9 "disadvantaged students" is not available.

Comparing percentages at lower and upper secondary levels (Table 4.10) shows a significant drop in percentages between the two levels in countries where comparative data are available (median lower secondary 2.14%, upper secondary 0.09%, Wilcoxon test $N = 9$ $T = 0$ $p<0.05$), with all countries showing the same trend.

Data on the location of the education of these students at upper secondary level are only available for seven countries, as shown in Chart 4.30 – they repeat the pattern found at primary and lower secondary – Belgium (Fl.), Canada (NB), Italy, the Netherlands and Turkey place all students receiving additional resources for social disadvantages in regular mainstream classes, while France has a small percentage (2%) in special classes, with the rest in regular classes. The Slovak Republic places all such students in special schools.

Table 4.10. Comparison of numbers of children with disadvantages receiving additional resources in lower and upper secondary education, as a percentage of all children in that phase of education

	Lower secondary	Upper secondary
Slovak Republic	0.13	0.11
Czech Republic	0.15	0.14
Poland	0.34	0.04
Spain	1.65	0.00
Italy	2.14	0.90
Canada (NB)	3.94	1.84
Netherlands	6.49	1.12
Belgium (Fl.)	6.77	3.11
France	13.88	3.43

Chart 4.30. **Percentages of students receiving additional resources in upper secondary education in cross-national category C by location[1, 2]**

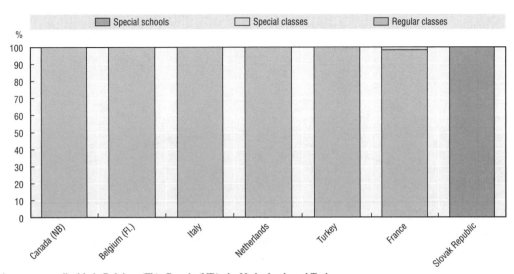

1. Special classes: not applicable in Belgium (Fl.), Canada (NB), the Netherlands and Turkey.
2. Special schools: not applicable in Belgium (Fl.), Canada (NB), France, Italy, the Netherlands and Turkey.

Overall comparisons across the phases of education for the three cross-national categories

Chart 4.31 compares the average percentage of students receiving additional resources at different levels or phases of education separately for students with disabilities, difficulties and disadvantages. In each case the average is for those countries for which data are available for all phases of education (including those countries where a particular category is not applicable or another known zero). As noted on the chart the countries contributing vary from A to B to C. However, if the analysis is restricted to the five countries for which data are available at all levels, and for each of the cross-national categories, as indicated in Chart 4.32, an identical pattern emerges. Note the caution expressed above in making comparisons between data relating to A and B on the one hand, and C on the other. However the main point of interest here is in making comparisons between the relative sizes of percentages through the educational system for A, B, and C separately.

Students with disabilities increase in proportion of the school population through pre-primary and primary, peaking at lower secondary, before falling away at upper secondary level. However, students with difficulties and those with disadvantages show a different common pattern, where the peak is reached earlier at primary level, then falling successively at lower and upper secondary levels.

Chart 4.31. **Mean number of students receiving additional resources at different levels of education by cross-national category, as a percentage of all students in that level of education**

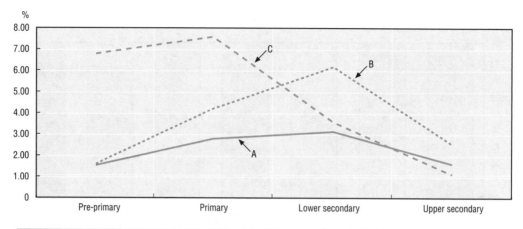

	Pre-primary	Primary	Lower secondary	Upper secondary
Category A	1.49	2.76	3.11	1.57
Category B	1.57	4.19	6.18	2.50
Category C	6.80	7.62	3.55	1.07

Chart 4.32. **Mean number of students receiving additional resources at different levels of education by cross-national category, as a percentage of all students in that level of education (restricted to countries with data at all levels and for each cross-national category)**

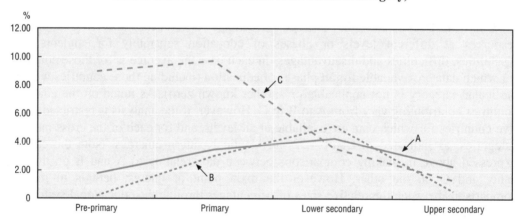

	Pre-primary	Primary	Lower secondary	Upper secondary
Category A	1.70	3.41	4.20	2.22
Category B	0.12	2.95	5.12	0.46
Category C	8.98	9.75	3.50	1.26

Chapter 5
Additional analyses of the quantitative data: gender and age

Introduction

This chapter focuses on what the data tables show about the different physical locations in which students receiving additional resources for disabilities, difficulties or disadvantages are educated. The simple categorisation, employed in the previous chapter, of special schools, special classes in mainstream schools, and regular classes in mainstream schools, is again used. Several other aspects are also analysed including the gender ratios for these students in different settings and categorisations, student-staff ratios and the age distributions of the students in a number of national systems.

Special schools

The amount of segregated provision in the form of special schools differs widely from country to country. As Table 5.1 shows the number of such institutions expressed as a proportion of the total school population over the period of compulsory education varies from 2.0 to 80.8 per 100 000 students, with a median value of 33.3 and quartile[1] values of 17.9 and 39.2 for the 13 countries for which data are available. There is considerable variation in school numbers both across levels and across countries. Canada (NB) has no special schools, while Italy has a very small number of special schools at all levels, with none exceeding 2 per 100 000. As noted above, provision is typically low at pre-school levels with the Netherlands providing an extreme outlier at 125.0.

Table 5.2 shows that the average size of special schools over the period of compulsory education varies substantially from country to country. The median value is 70 students per school, with quartiles at 44.8 and 123.7. The lowest average size is in Mexico (12.5 students per school) with Greece also averaging fewer than 20 students per school. Five countries average over 100 students per school, Hungary with the largest at 148.5.

Pre-primary centres are very small (median value 13.8), ranging in size from 5.4 (Greece) to 23.0 (Slovak Republic). Special schools at primary level are somewhat larger (median size 29.6; quartiles at 24.0 and 94.5). For countries where data are available for both pre-primary and primary levels, the latter are all larger (dramatically so in the case of Belgium [Fl.], Belgium [Fr.] and the Netherlands). Sizes at lower secondary are slightly larger (median 44.6), although there is considerable variation, with three countries showing a decrease and three an increase when comparative data are available. There is also some tendency for sizes to increase at upper secondary level (median value 67.2), but no consistent pattern across countries. The relative proportions of male and female students in special schools are discussed in a separate section below.

---

1. See Footnote 1, Chapter 4.

Table 5.1. **Number of special schools by level of education relative to total school population**[1,2,3,4,5]

	Compulsory education	Pre-primary	Primary	Lower secondary	Upper secondary
Belgium (Fl.)	36.5	33.3	44.5	27.0	
Belgium (Fr.)	33.3	50.9	46.0	76.7	
Czech Republic	80.8				49.0
Germany	26.8	17.3			
Greece	19.4	26.5	22.3		
Hungary	15.1	18.5	13.4		
Italy		0.6	1.7	0.5	0.2
Japan		8.9			18.8
Mexico	61.3				
Netherlands	35.5	125.0	64.1		
Slovak Republic	39.2	40.3	94.6	72.7	21.2
Spain	10.8				
Switzerland	45.9				
Turkey	2.0	11.6	2.0		0.4
United Kingdom (Eng.)	17.9				

1. In Belgium (Fl.) and Belgium (Fr.) upper secondary data are included in lower secondary.
2. In Turkey data are for public schools only at primary and upper secondary level.
3. In Spain the figure in compulsory education includes all levels of education (ISCED 0, 1, 2, 3).
4. Number per 100 000 of total school population at that level.
5. Data are only presented in this table if it is possible to give a non-zero value (*i.e.* it is not available, not applicable, included in other values, or there are no schools at this level).

Table 5.2. **Size of special schools by level of education**[1,2,3]

	Compulsory education	Pre-primary	Primary	Lower secondary	Upper secondary
Belgium (Fl.)	137.2	19.3	136.3	138.8	
Belgium (Fr.)	120.1	12.2	93.7	139.0	
Czech Republic	47.0	17.1	26.7	22.3	71.1
Germany	134.6	17.8			
Greece	18.6	5.4	20.2		
Hungary	148.5	17.2			
Italy		15.4	25.2	16.5	63.2
Japan		10.4			50.2
Mexico	12.5	9.0	12.8		
Netherlands	108.8	9.7	96.9	44.6	33.4
Slovak Republic	75.6	23.0	32.4	44.6	81.9
Spain	55.6				
Switzerland	38.2				
Turkey		10.4			86.6
United Kingdom (Eng.)	64.4				

1. In Belgium (Fl.) and Belgium (Fr.) upper secondary data are included in lower secondary.
2. In Turkey data are for public schools only at primary and upper secondary levels.
3. In Spain the figure in compulsory education includes all levels of education (ISCED 0, 1, 2, 3).

In most countries the overwhelming proportion of special schools are publicly provided as indicated in Table 5.3 (median value 92.0%, quartiles at 51.5% and 95.9%) over the period of compulsory education.

Table 5.3. **Percentage of public special schools[1, 2]**

	Compulsory education	Pre-primary	Primary	Lower secondary	Upper secondary
Belgium (Fl.)	35.0	35.8	35.1	34.8	
Belgium (Fr.)	45.3	55.0	53.3	42.4	
Czech Republic	93.2	89.1	93.1	94.2	92.1
Germany	83.2	95.2			
Hungary	92.0	91.2	92.0		
Italy	100	100.0	100.0	100.0	100.0
Mexico	99.6	99.9	99.8		
Slovak Republic	98.3	96.8	98.2	98.3	100.0
Spain	40.3				
Switzerland	57.7				
United Kingdom (Eng.)	93.5				

1. In Belgium (Fl.) and Belgium (Fr.) upper secondary data are included in lower secondary.
2. In Spain the figure in compulsory education includes all levels of education (ISCED 0, 1, 2, 3).

In Belgium (Fl.) and Spain approximately 60% of the special schools are private over the period of compulsory education, while in Belgium (Fr.) there is a nearly 50/50 public/private split at all levels of education. Where data are available for different phases of education, the percentage of private schools is remarkably consistent over phases in a particular country.

Special classes

Data on special classes are sparse compared with those available on special schools. Only five countries provide data which permit the number of special classes per school for students receiving additional resources for disabilities, difficulties or disadvantages as shown in Table 5.4. Figures for the compulsory education period range from 3.8 in the Czech Republic to one class per school in Greece. The most typical figure at all levels of education is one class per school. Average class sizes, also shown in Table 5.4 are, in most cases, small – typically about 10 students per class. Italy has very small class sizes at all levels. There are insufficient data to make comparisons between class sizes at different phases of education. Gender ratios in special classes are also discussed separately below.

Table 5.4. **Number and size of special classes**

Average number of special classes per school

	Compulsory education	Pre-primary	Primary	Lower secondary	Upper secondary
Czech Republic	3.8	1.3	2.7	2.7	1.0
Greece	1.0	1.0	1.0	1.0	
Hungary	2.9		2.9		
Italy		1.0	2.0	3.5	1.0
Slovak Republic	2.2	1.3			4.0

Table 5.4. **Number and size of special classes** *(continued)*

Average size of special classes

	Compulsory education	Pre-primary	Primary	Lower secondary	Upper secondary
Czech Republic	11.7	11.4	11.2	12.4	9.0
Greece	13.6	3.4	14.0	9.2	
Hungary	10.5		10.5		
Italy		5.0	4.2	4.9	5.0
Slovak Republic	9.9	10.7	9.7	10.1	8.5
Switzerland	9.5				
Turkey	9.9		9.9		

Regular classes

Information about the integrated provision made when students receiving additional resources for disabilities, difficulties or disadvantages are educated in the same classes as other students is crucial in any assessment of this type of provision. Unfortunately, it appears that this kind of information remains rarely available at national level when statistics are collected. In the current exercise only a few countries were able to provide a complete set of relevant data as given in Table 5.5. Italy and the Canadian province of New Brunswick are both jurisdictions with a policy of full inclusion and it is clear that a very substantial number of classes are involved, with multiple classes at all levels. The numbers of classes per school with students receiving additional resources increases markedly at upper secondary level in Canada (NB), possibly linked to the much larger average size of schools at this level. Gender ratios for students with special educational needs in regular classes are discussed below.

Table 5.5. **Number of regular classes with students receiving additional resources**

Number of classes

	Compulsory education	Pre-primary	Primary	Lower secondary	Upper secondary
Canada (NB)	517		259	113	145
Italy		11 757	45 147	35 528	16 506
Czech Republic	23 663	1 776	12 190	11 473	479
Turkey	5 728		5 728		684

Average number of classes per school

	Compulsory education	Pre-primary	Primary	Lower secondary	Upper secondary
Canada (NB)	15.2		10.8	11.3	20.7
Italy		2.0	3.4	5.5	4.7

Student/staff ratios

Teaching and other staff are some of the most important resources made available to support the education of students with disabilities, learning difficulties and disadvantages. While it was felt to be highly desirable to collect data about support staff of various kinds, the pilot work on the development of the data collection instrument (discussed in the earlier monograph, OECD, 2000b) established that this information was rarely available at national level. It appeared that there was a somewhat greater availability of data on teachers themselves. Table 5.6 gathers the available data on special schools, special classes and regular classes respectively. The ratios in special schools, ranging from 3.5 to 11.7 for the period of compulsory education (median value 5.3; quartiles 4.9 and 6.9) are clearly highly favourable compared to those in regular education. Directly comparable figures are not available but OECD figures for education as a whole show ranges from 10.0 to 32.1 at primary level, and ranges from 9.3 to 29.2 at lower secondary level. As figures for the compulsory education period might be expected to fall between those for primary and lower secondary, this strongly suggests that there is little or no overlap between the distribution of student/staff ratios in special schools and regular education.

Table 5.6.   **Student/teacher ratios**

Special schools[1,2]

	Compulsory education	Pre-primary	Primary	Lower secondary	Upper secondary
Belgium (Fl.)	5.0	4.4	6.3	3.7	
Belgium (Fr.)	4.3				
Czech Republic	6.9	5.8	6.9	6.9	11.2
Germany	6.9				
Greece	3.5	3.9	3.8	2.1	
Hungary	5.2	4.8	5.2		
Italy		2.3	2.1	0.9	2.1
Mexico	8.1	8.3	9.3		
Slovak Republic	6.7	5.8	7.4	6.3	10.3
Spain	4.7				
Turkey	11.7	14.2	11.7		12.0
United Kingdom (Eng.)	5.3				

1. For Spain the figure in compulsory education includes all levels of education (pre-primary, primary, lower secondary and upper secondary).
2. For Belgium (Fl.) and Belgium (Fr.) upper secondary data are included in lower secondary.

Special classes

	Compulsory education	Pre-primary	Primary	Lower secondary	Upper secondary
Czech Republic	8.8	5.9	10.1	7.4	2.3
Greece	12.0	3.4	14.0	0.9	
Hungary	9.4		9.4		
Slovak Republic	7.6	5.7	8.4	6.8	3.8
Turkey	9.8		9.8		

Table 5.6. **Student/teacher ratios** *(continued)*

All classes[1, 2, 3, 4]

	Pre-primary education	Primary education	Lower secondary education	Upper secondary education
Belgium	16.7	13.4		
Canada	11.5	18.3	18.4	17.2
Czech Republic	12.7	19.4	14.5	13.1
Finland	13.0	16.1	10.9	17.0
France	19.2	19.5	13.5	11.2
Germany	24.6	19.4	15.7	13.7
Greece	14.5	12.7	9.8	9.7
Hungary	11.4	11.3	11.2	12.5
Italy	12.8	10.8	9.9	10.4
Japan	18.5	20.6	16.6	14.0
Korea	22.2	32.1	21.0	19.3
Mexico	21.9	27.0	29.2	23.8
Netherlands		17.2		
Poland	12.8	12.5	13.1	16.8
Slovak Republic	10.0	20.7	14.5	12.9
Spain	16.0	14.7		
Sweden	10.3	12.4	12.4	16.6
Turkey	15.6	29.8		17.2
United Kingdom (Eng.)	22.1	20.5	17.3	12.3
United States	14.9	16.3	17.0	14.8

1. In Switzerland data refer to public institutions only.
2. In the United Kingdom (Eng.) data include only general programmes at upper secondary education.
3. For Belgium, Finland, Hungary, Italy, the Netherlands, Spain and Sweden, see Annex 3 in OECD (2003a).
4. Data are only presented in this table if it is possible to give a non-zero value.

For the seven countries for which some comparative data across levels are available no consistent pattern emerges. Ratios in Turkey typically exceed 10, while Mexico is slightly smaller. At the other end are found Greece with ratios around 3, and Italy with the lowest ratios, typically hardly above 2, at all levels.

Student/teacher ratios in special classes are very similar, with a tendency to be somewhat higher than in special schools. They range from 7.6 to 12.0 for the period of compulsory education (median value 9.4).

Relative numbers of male and female students receiving additional resources for disabilities, difficulties or disadvantages

A strong and consistent finding reported in the earlier monographs (OECD, 2000b, pp. 91-94; OECD, 2003b; OECD, 2004, pp. 109-113) was the preponderance of the number of males over females in a wide range of analyses. Whether done by location (special schools, special classes, regular classes), cross-national or national category, age of student, or stage of education there was a higher percentage of males – typically approximating to a 60/40 split.

Tables 5.7 to 5.9 show gender ratios from the latest data collection exercise, focusing on location and cross-national category analyses. The earlier finding is fully replicated. With a small number of isolated exceptions there are more boys than girls receiving additional resources in all three cross-national categories and at all locations at which they receive education.

Table 5.7. **Gender ratios of students receiving additional resources for disabilities (cross-national category A)**

Table values are percentage of males[1,2,3]

Special schools	Compulsory education	Pre-primary	Primary	Lower secondary	Upper secondary
Belgium (Fl.)	60.2	66.6	59.2	60.5	
Belgium (Fr.)	63.9	61.0	63.1	64.5	
Czech Republic	58.4		58.2	58.3	61.1
Finland					60.1
Germany	62.7				
Hungary	59.9	63.5	59.9	59.8	
Italy		67.5	63.5	53.7	59.8
Japan	53.8	51.4	57.6	55.9	63.2
Mexico	59.6	59.2	59.6	60.0	
Netherlands	69.2	69.4	68.9	70.4	62.8
Poland		56.1			58.5
Slovak Republic	56.1	56.2	56.7	55.7	57.7
Spain	61.4	61.5	61.4	60.7	
Switzerland	61.9				
Turkey	63.6	58.5	63.6		72.4
United Kingdom (Eng.)	68.8	64.5	69.1	69.1	65.5

1. In Belgium (Fl.) and Belgium (Fr.) upper secondary data are included in lower secondary.
2. In Japan the data refer only to the blind and partially sighted, and the deaf and partially hearing.
3. In Turkey primary data do not include category 8 "chronic illness".

Special classes	Compulsory education	Pre-primary	Primary	Lower secondary	Upper secondary
Czech Republic	59.3		58.9	59.8	33.3
Finland					59.5
Hungary	59.2		59.5	58.8	
Italy		40.0	62.6	69.6	60.0
Mexico	62.0	69.7	61.9	68.9	
Slovak Republic	54.3	56.4	57.0	51.4	29.4
Turkey	60.6		60.6		

Regular classes	Compulsory education	Pre-primary	Primary	Lower secondary	Upper secondary
Canada (NB)	64.2		66.4	62.7	63.2
Czech Republic	60.8		58.5	64.1	72.7
Mexico	60.7	65.2	60.7	61.1	
Spain	60.7	60.6	61.0	60.2	60.7
Turkey	62.1	62.4	62.1		62.9
United Kingdom (Eng.)	68.8	64.5	69.1	69.0	65.5

Table 5.8.   **Gender ratios of students receiving additional resources for difficulties (cross-national category B)**

Table values are percentage of males

Special schools	Compulsory education	Pre-primary	Primary	Lower secondary	Upper secondary
Belgium (Fl.)	69.1	77.0	67.5	84.4	83.5
Belgium (Fr.)	63.9	60.8	63.3	65.8	
Czech Republic	71.4		71.9	70.6	
Finland					74.7
France	61.7		55.6	62.4	61.3
Germany	64.0	63.5			
Hungary	64.5	53.2	63.3	67.9	
Mexico	66.5	59.0	64.6	77.1	
Netherlands	68.0	73.5	67.9		
United Kingdom (Eng.)	69.0	64.3	69.1	69.4	65.9

Special classes	Compulsory education	Pre-primary	Primary	Lower secondary	Upper secondary
Czech Republic	71.0		70.0	72.3	
Finland					69.7
France			58.9	58.9	
Hungary	59.3		59.5	57.8	
Mexico	62.0	69.7	61.9	69.0	
Netherlands	61.7			61.7	
Slovak Republic	65.2	71.4	66.2	64.0	
Switzerland	61.8				

Regular classes	Compulsory education	Pre-primary	Primary	Lower secondary	Upper secondary
Canada (NB)	76.5		80.2	79.6	65.3
Czech Republic	72.8		70.8	74.9	66.7
Finland					74.5
Mexico	53.7	67.2	60.2	63.5	
Spain	58.6	63.4	61.7	55.0	60.1
Turkey	61.3	80.0	61.3		47.4
United Kingdom (Eng.)	68.9	64.5	69.1	69.0	65.5

Inspection of the data shows that, for disabilities and difficulties, the percentage of males is typically between 60% and 70%, while for disadvantages it is typically between 50% and 60%. For students with disabilities exceptions are rare. All the countries report usable data, and 53 data points fall within the remarkably small range of 55.7% to 72.4%. In special classes and regular classes a few ratios of less than 50% are reported with Italy at 40% males in pre-primary special classes and the Slovak Republic at 29.4% at upper secondary level.

Table 5.9.   **Gender ratios of students receiving additional resources for disadvantages (cross-national category C)**

Table values are percentage of males

Special schools	Compulsory education	Pre-primary	Primary	Lower secondary	Upper secondary
Czech Republic	72.3		70.5	70.3	75.5
Mexico	51.9	50.0	51.9		
Poland					54.8
Slovak Republic	77.7	52.6	79.1	78.1	57.8
Turkey	60.0		60.0		

Special classes	Compulsory education	Pre-primary	Primary	Lower secondary	Upper secondary
Belgium (Fl.)				53.7	
Switzerland	53.1				

Regular classes	Compulsory education	Pre-primary	Primary	Lower secondary	Upper secondary
Belgium (Fr.)					52.3
Canada (NB)	74.7		78.2	79.8	61.5
Italy		55.4	53.9	55.7	49.8
Netherlands	50.4	51.2	50.2	51.6	49.7
Spain	55.2	53.0	54.3	58.8	
Turkey	57.8	68.8	57.8		55.1

Ratios for students with difficulties or disadvantages show a greater degree of variability. The Czech Republic typically report over 70% males with learning difficulties in all settings and most levels of education. While percentages of male and female students with disadvantages is closer to equality, only 2 of 34 data points show more females than males, with the lowest male percentage still only just below 50%. Canada (NB) stands out as having approximately three-quarters of male students with disadvantages in regular schools at primary and lower secondary levels.

Charts 5.1 and 5.2 focus on the location of their education (for the period of compulsory education for which, as revealed in the tables, more countries are able to provide data than for the other phases of education) and the phase of education (across all locations of their education) respectively. The charts have to be viewed with some caution as there is variation in the countries contributing to the different data points in the charts. Also the number of countries contributing to data points in Chart 5.2 is, in some cases, as low as three.

It would clearly be preferable for analyses to be in all cases based on the same set of countries, particularly as inspection of the tables shows considerable country to country variability. Unfortunately the amount of missing data is such that restricting the analysis in this way in most cases results in there being too few countries for meaningful comparisons to be made.

Chart 5.1.   **Gender ratio by location and cross-national category (period of compulsory education)**

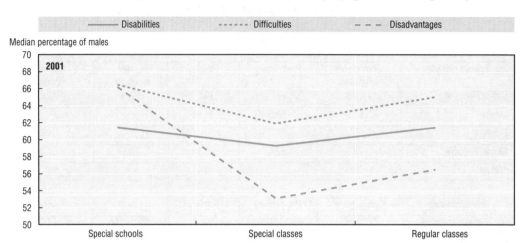

Chart 5.2.   **Gender ratio by phase of education and cross-national category (special schools, special classes and regular classes combined)**

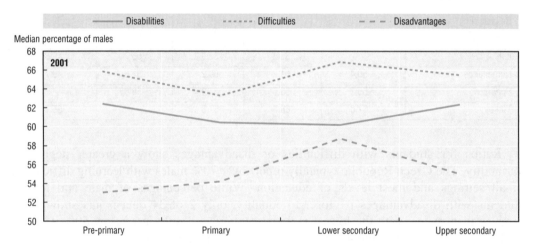

An exception occurs when comparing gender ratios in special schools. The percentage of males is smaller for students receiving additional resources for disabilities than for those receiving additional resources for difficulties (Tables 5.7 and 5.8). Median values are 61.4% (disabilities) and 67.2% (difficulties) over the period of compulsory education, the difference in percentages being statistically significant (Wilcoxon test, $n = 8$, $T = 0$, $p<0.05$). This difference is consistent across all phases of education (pre-primary 62.8% and 66.7%; primary 61.5% and 68.3%; lower secondary 62.1% and 71.8%; upper secondary 60.1% and 70.5% – differences statistically significant at primary and lower secondary levels). This corroborates the pattern found in Chart 5.2.

There are tantalising indications of other interesting patterns in the data. It is still considered premature to speculate on the interpretation of gender ratios at this time. A more extensive database will help to understand what lies behind this strong finding of males having greater access to additional resources provided to access the curriculum. The need is to move beyond the overall finding of a broad 60/40 male/female split. Consistent findings of higher and lower ratios, or of variability of ratios, with particular categories, settings, phases of education, or countries, when linked to knowledge about these categories, settings, etc., could provide the key to identifying the mechanisms at work in these contexts in producing this important social and educational phenomenon.

Given the importance of this issue, not least from an equity perspective, there is a strong case for all countries to collect gender information on all students receiving additional resources to access the curriculum.

Age distribution of students receiving additional resources for disabilities, difficulties or disadvantages

The charts are derived from Table 6 of the data collection exercise which asks for data on students in all categories falling within the resources definition by age; *i.e.* it effectively sums across cross-national categories A, B and C. Cohort size is taken into account so that the figures presented are percentages of students in each age group.

Nineteen of the 24 countries presenting data were able to provide some form of breakdown by age of students with special educational needs. Fourteen countries provided data on special schools and eleven on special classes.

Charts 5.3 and 5.4 illustrate the age distributions for special schools and special classes, respectively. Where gender data are available these are incorporated into the charts. It is once again noteworthy that the approximate 60/40 male/female split, discussed above in the section on gender breakdowns, remains strongly in evidence in the age breakdown data.

For special schools (Chart 5.3) for most countries the charts reveal a steady increase in the proportions of students in special schools from four years of age onwards. The charts rise to a peak and then decline rather sharply. The peak is commonly around 14/15 years of age although there is some variation among countries. There are two notable exceptions; Japan and Mexico. In Japan, the curve stays relatively flat until the age of 14/15 when there is a sharp rise in the proportion of students in special schools. In Mexico, the proportions decline steadily.

The data for special classes (Chart 5.4) reveal more complex patterns. Some countries show proportions rising to a peak and rapidly declining as in the special school data. Japan has a relatively flat curve and yet others, *e.g.* France and Switzerland, show an increase followed by a rapid decline followed by a second increase.

Although it is necessary to remain cautious about interpreting those data, a first attempt is made in the following paragraphs.

For those countries showing increases over time, it seems likely that this reflects the way in which countries cope with students who present difficulties of one sort or another to the school, *i.e.* students are progressively referred to special education systems from regular education systems as their needs become more and more difficult to cope with in regular schools. In Mexico it seems likely that as students get older they progressively leave special schools and up to age 8 at least may be transferred to special classes. What happens after that age in that country remains unclear.

Chart 5.3. **Numbers of students receiving additional resources in special schools as a proportion of all students by age, 2001**

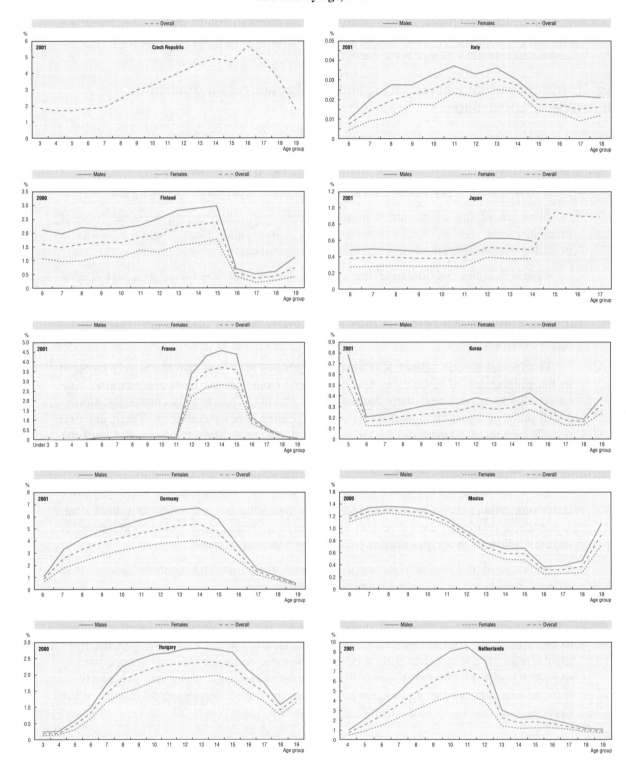

Chart 5.3. **Numbers of students receiving additional resources in special schools as a proportion of all students by age, 2001** *(continued)*

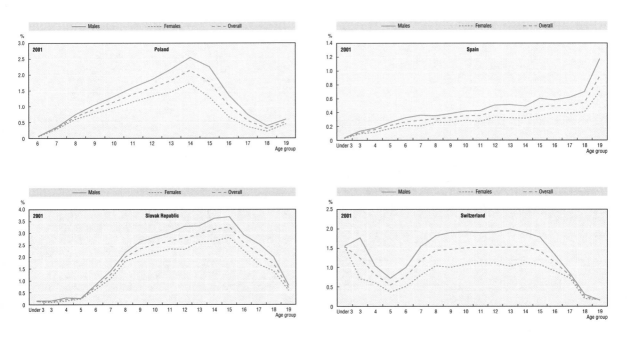

Chart 5.4. **Numbers of students receiving additional resources in special classes as a proportion of all students by age, 2001**

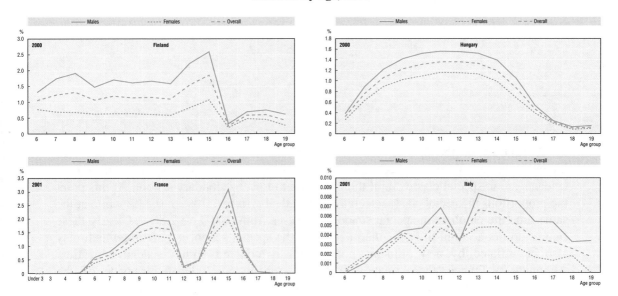

Chart 5.4. **Numbers of students receiving additional resources in special classes as a proportion of all students by age, 2001** *(continued)*

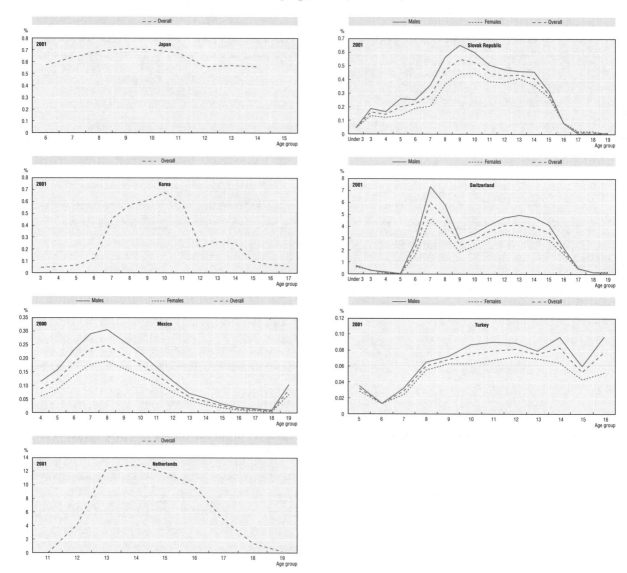

A contrast of the special school and special class data for France reveals an interesting story. Within the education system it appears that the majority of A type students are in special classes until the transition to lower secondary school. At this point the proportions in special classes decrease dramatically from 1.70% to 0.24% while at the same time the numbers in special schools increases from 0.01% to 2.86%. Clearly these figures do not account fully for the increase in the special school population which may also be inflated by new students not previously counted within special education. Although in France approximately 0.8% of students are educated outside of the educational system, in this provision the proportions steadily increase over time (see Chart 5.5) and the new numbers in special schools do not match with an equivalent decrease in the non-registered student numbers. On the other hand it does seem likely that the relatively low proportions of students in special schools in the primary years may be linked to the provision made by the Health Ministry.

Students not registered within the education system

In the data collection exercise reported here an additional question was asked in Table 6 on the "total number of students not registered within the educational system administered by the Ministry of Education". Previous discussions indicated that there were such students in some countries. Their existence, in some countries but not others, is a potential biasing factor when making national comparisons.

Unfortunately, only one country, France, was able to provide relevant data, shown in Chart 5.5. Data returns indicated that in several other countries there were such students but the relevant data were not available.

Chart 5.5. **Age distribution of students not registered within the education system[1]**

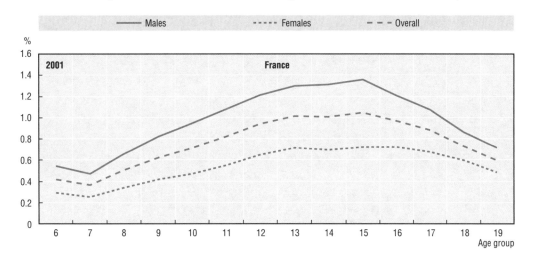

1. Students not administered by the Ministry of Education.

It is clear that there may be a substantial biasing factor arising from the indication that almost one third of the countries involved in this data collection exercise may be excluding an unknown number of students from the returns made, who in other countries may well be included in their returns. Whereas in some countries all students receiving additional resources for disabilities, difficulties or disadvantages are the responsibility of a ministry or department of education and/or are included in the return made by this ministry, in other countries for organisational or historical reasons some of these students are the responsibility of other ministries and may not be included in the returns made.

Overall discussion

The chapter provides useful descriptive information about the amount and nature of the provision in different countries for students receiving additional resources for disabilities, difficulties or disadvantages. As established in the earlier monographs (OECD, 2000b, 2003b, 2004) and confirmed here, there are generally high quality data on aspects of special school systems.

However, although the data coverage is somewhat greater than that found in the previous exercises, few countries are able to provide substantial amounts of data on provision in special classes.

While there are data on gender ratios, discussed in some detail above, it is not yet available from many countries which hampers attempts to provide convincing explanations for the over-representation of males amongst students receiving additional resources, particularly in connection with disabilities or difficulties.

Chapter 6
Further discussion of significant issues

This chapter draws together the main outcomes presented in the monograph. It analyses cross-national categories A, B and C separately and, through consideration of other CERI work (*e.g.* OECD, 1999), discusses their policy implications. A final section reviews the experience of the last rounds of data collection and in the light of this identifies needed future developments.

It is clear that countries provide substantial additional support for many students in order to help them access the curriculum. The significance of the issue is reflected in the many laws, policies and types of special education provision developed to meet these students' educational needs. Factors repeatedly identified by countries which serve as facilitators for or barriers to equity and inclusion include legal frameworks, funding models, assessment arrangements, school structure, class size, the use of individual teaching programmes, the involvement of additional teachers and aides, teacher training, parental involvement and co-operation with other services. Taken together, these issues present a considerable agenda for reform.

The work also shows the wide variation between countries in the conceptual frameworks that are used to classify these students. The differences are exhibited in Table 2.2 where national definitions for each category are laid out. Apart from the inherent interest in the different models used in countries, the table immediately shows the difficulties in making comparisons between countries for these students. Nevertheless, countries welcomed these data displays and analyses and Chapter 2 therefore provides data for those categories where there is most confidence of comparability between countries. Despite their controversial nature these data are included to give a sense of connection with the way in which countries gather their own data. National data sets (1999) are published on the Internet, *www.oecd.org/edu/equity/senddd*

What emerges most strongly from these data presentations is the large between country variation in prevalence rates. The complexity in variation in funding systems for these students among countries makes interpretation of these results difficult and points to the need for more detailed information to be gathered. The launching of work in individual schools should help to clarify this finding. The substantial variations at different levels of education and degree of difference in the place of education – special school, special class or regular class – are also noteworthy.

Chapter 4 presents the data broken down by cross-national categories A, B and C for students with disabilities, difficulties and disadvantages. This procedure allows for all national variations in the concept of special education and definitions in use to be taken into account. It has the effect of smoothing the data to some extent to improve comparability.

Alternative explanations of these findings are discussed in the next section.

Issues arising from the analyses of the cross-national category A, B and C data

The results of the analyses presented above raise many issues which are discussed below for A, B and C in turn. They are expressed in terms of a set of questions followed by a set of tentative answers and policy action implications. The discussion applies equally to the data presented in Chapter 3, which are used to elaborate answers where relevant. It needs to be emphasised that every effort has been made to ensure that the classification of national data into the cross-national categories of A, B and C is valid and reliable. The classifications provided have been agreed at meetings of national representatives and while the possibility remains that errors exist they are assumed to be minimal.

Cross-national category A – students receiving additional resources for disabilities

1. Why does the percentage of students receiving additional resources for disabilities differ from country to country?

When the number of students receiving additional resources for disabilities is expressed as a percentage of all students there is considerable country to country variation. The range is from below 1% to above 4% for all phases of education. Suggestions as to possible factors or mechanisms underlying these differences follow, with a commentary. There is, of course, no suggestion that a single factor or mechanism is involved.

- *Differences reflect differential incidence or prevalence of disabilities.* While such a possibility cannot be discounted, it is perhaps best addressed at the level of specific disabilities such as blindness. It is clear that there are large between country variations in prevalence in individual disability categories.

- *Some countries provide additional resources for disabilities which are not so resourced in other countries.* Inspection of Table 2.2 in Chapter 2 reveals the difficulties involved in assessing this possibility. The number, labelling, and definition of categories of disability vary widely from country to country in a manner which obscures any linkage with overall proportions of students given additional resources.

- *Some countries do not provide additional resources for disabilities at particular phases of education.* Thus Ireland appears not to provide additional resources for disabilities at pre-primary level.

- *Differences reflect policy differences.* Some countries, for instance for reasons of equity, may make the additional resources for students with disabilities an educational priority. Note that this is not a simple question of the relative wealth of countries. The very high United Kingdom (Eng) percentage at pre-primary and upper secondary (relative both to other countries, and to United Kingdom [Eng] percentages for the middle years of schooling) may well represent policy considerations.

2. Why do some countries educate virtually all students receiving additional resources for disabilities in regular classes with other students, while other countries educate virtually all of them in special schools?

Inspection of the relevant charts in Chapter 3 shows that, while Canada (NB) educates virtually all students receiving additional resources for disabilities alongside their non-disabled peers, several other countries educate over 80% of them in segregated special schools. However a majority of countries operate a form of mixed economy involving substantial use of regular classrooms together with special schools and/or special classes.

- Differences reflect *policy differences*. It appears highly likely that inclusion or segregation is a matter of national policy in contrast for instance to being a parental decision.

- *There are features of mainstream schools and their curriculum, and the attitudes of their teachers, which facilitate or obstruct integration.* Study of these features is a priority.

- *There are features of special schools, and of other segregated provision, which are viewed as desirable by educators and parents.* Study of these features is also a priority.

Policy action implications

Given the increased costs of special provision for these groups (at least twice that for non-disabled students, OECD, 1999) countries should carefully review how students become labelled as disabled and how decisions are made about their placement. In addition reviews of the preparation of professionals are called for to serve as a budget neutral preventive mechanism (see OECD, 1999).

Cross-national category B – students receiving additional resources for difficulties

3. Why do some countries have no national categories falling within cross-national category B (i.e. they appear not to be providing additional resources for students with difficulties)?

All countries providing data in this exercise have national categories falling within cross-national category A. The obvious interpretation is that all countries have within their educational system students who have disabilities, and all countries recognise that such students require additional resources to access the regular curriculum.

However, as made clear in Chapter 1, in 2001 some countries (Italy, Japan, Poland) had no national categories falling within cross-national category B. (Turkey only has students described as "gifted and talented".[1]) The interpretation of this fact is more problematic. Possibilities, of varying degrees of plausibility, include:

- *The curriculum is such that no students (other than those with disabilities or social disadvantages) have difficulty in accessing it.* While this possibility appears close to utopian it would be of great interest if any countries making this claim

---

1. Students considered to be gifted and talented are not discussed in this monograph.

could explain how their educational system effectively eliminates behaviour, learning and other difficulties affecting access to the regular curriculum.

- *Students have difficulties but additional resources are not provided.* If this explanation is put forward it is reasonable to request a rationale. Note that if there are national categories of difficulties for which no additional resources are provided they are expected to have been declared in the data collection exercise (and further declared as falling outside the resources definition).

- *Students have difficulties and additional resources are provided but relevant data are not available to data providers.* If this is the case the expectation is that appropriate categories falling within B are declared in the data collection exercise and coded as "data not available". This provides a flag that the data are out there somewhere and indicates that a different methodology of data collection (perhaps more locally based) may have to be employed. Alternatively, the data may be collected by some other agency than that directly responsible for the provision of data, calling for cross-agency liaison.

- *Countries are not prepared to declare national categories falling within B for educational, policy or other reasons.* Such possibilities are recognised and respected. However, the data collection exercise is not dependent on the existence of national categories. If it is accepted that students have difficulties in gaining access to the regular curriculum and additional resources are made available to support such students, it would be expected that some form of classification would be adopted to either allocate, or account for, such resources.

4. Why does the percentage of students receiving additional resources for difficulties differ more widely from country to country than for disabilities?

The range for difficulties is typically from 0% to above 10% for all phases of education although reaching above 25% in some countries in some phases of education (compared to about half this range with disabilities).

- *Some countries which do provide additional resources for difficulties do so for large percentages of students.* When combined with the fact that some countries have no cross-national category B provision this results in large ranges across countries. Factors possibly underlying this are discussed below.

5. Why does the percentage of students receiving additional resources for difficulties differ from country to country?

This is the same question discussed above in Section 1 in the context of disabilities (indeed it is a question arising in most aspects of the analysis of the data collected in this exercise – with the exception of gender ratios). Given that issues concerning those countries with no cross-national category B students have been discussed above in Section 3, this discussion focuses on differences in percentages between countries with such students.

- *Some countries provide additional resources for difficulties which are not so resourced in other countries.* Inspection of Table 2.2 in Chapter 2 again illustrates the problems involved in assessing this possibility. The number, labelling, and definition of categories of difficulties vary widely from country to country in a manner which obscures any linkage with overall proportions of students given additional resources.

- *Differences reflect policy differences*. Some countries may make the additional resourcing of students with difficulties an educational priority. The existence of large numbers of students perceived as needing additional resources because of behavioural, emotional or other difficulties in accessing the regular curriculum may be seen positively as indexing sensitivity to such problems, or negatively as a function of a mismatch of curriculum provision and the needs of the student.

- *Some countries' regular systems deal better with individual differences and minimise the need for differentiation.*

6. Why do some countries educate virtually all students receiving additional resources for difficulties in regular classes with other students, while other countries educate virtually all of them in special schools or classes?

Inspection of the relevant charts in Chapter 3 shows that, while many countries educate virtually all students receiving additional resources for difficulties in fully integrated settings, several other countries educate virtually all of them in special schools or special classes. While data availability is patchier than for students with disabilities (where most countries operated a mixed economy distributing students with disabilities between special schools, special classes or regular classes), the picture here is more dichotomous with a substantial majority of students at all phases of education being typically either in integrated settings or in special schools or classes.

- *Differences reflect policy differences*. It appears highly likely that integration or segregation is a matter of national policy.

- *There are features of mainstream schools and their curriculum, and the attitudes of their teachers, which facilitate or obstruct integration.* Study of these features is a priority.

- *There are features of special schools and classes, which are viewed as desirable by educators and parents.* Study of these features is also a priority.

Policy action implications

Students who generally fall into category B are those who should be able to receive their education in mainstream schools given relevant changes to the way the regular schools function. The fact that many countries educate these students in special schools or classes also requires review. It is possible that those countries having no "B" students include them in categories that are otherwise placed in either A or C. If they fall into A and special school or special class provision is made this is likely to be prejudicial to the students' life chances and hence inequitable.

Countries need to carefully review their decision-making procedures with regard to these students as well as other school based and professional preparation factors. These aspects may well lead unnecessarily to inappropriate and costly labelling. It may also be the case, that there are students who fall into this category who are unidentified and may, as a result, be inadequately resourced.

Cross-national category C – students receiving additional resources for disadvantages

7. Why do some countries have no national categories falling within cross-national category C (i.e. they appear not to be providing additional resources for students with disadvantages)?

This discussion and analysis mirror that presented in Section 3 above considering cross-national category B.

Some countries have no national categories falling within cross-national category C. Again interpretation of this fact is problematic, with possibilities including:

- *The curriculum is such that students with social disadvantages have no particular problems in accessing it.*

- *The social system is such that no students are disadvantaged to the extent that they have problems in accessing the regular curriculum.* While these possibilities again appear close to utopian it would be of great interest if any countries making either or both of these claims could explain how their educational and/or social systems effectively eliminate social disadvantage affecting access to the regular curriculum.

- *Students have disadvantages but additional resources are not provided.* If this explanation is put forward it is again reasonable to request a rationale. Note that if there are national categories of disadvantages for which no additional resources are provided they are expected to have been declared in the data collection exercise (and further declared as falling outside the resources definition).

- *Students have disadvantages and additional resources are provided but relevant data are not available to data providers.* If this is the case the expectation is that appropriate categories falling within C are declared in the data collection exercise and coded as "data not available". This provides a flag that the data are out there somewhere and indicates that a different methodology of data collection (perhaps more locally based) may have to be employed. Alternatively, the data may be collected by some other agency than that directly responsible for the provision of data, calling for cross-agency liaison.

- *Countries are not prepared to declare national categories falling within C for educational, political or other reasons.* Such possibilities are again recognised and respected. However, the data collection exercise is not dependent on the existence of national categories. If it is accepted that students have disadvantages in gaining access to the regular curriculum and additional resources are made available to support such students, it would be expected that some form of classification would be adopted to either allocate, or account for, such resources.

8. Why does the percentage of students receiving additional resources for disadvantages differ more widely from country to country than for disabilities?

The range for disadvantages is typically from 0% to above 10% for all phases of education (although it is substantially higher, approaching 35% in some countries) apart from upper secondary (compared to about half this range with disabilities).

- *Some countries which do provide additional resources for disadvantages do so for large percentages of students.* When combined with the fact that some countries have no cross-national category C provision this results in large ranges across countries. Factors possibly underlying this are discussed below.

- *The basis for computing student numbers involved may differ from that in cross-national category A.* As discussed earlier in the chapter, numbers of students receiving additional resources for disabilities (and also for difficulties) are typically based on head-counts. All such students need these resources to access the regular curriculum. Numbers of students with social and other disadvantages may be computed on a group or class basis where the resources are provided for all falling within that classification irrespective of the needs of specific individuals. In these circumstances an inflated figure (compared with that for disabilities or disadvantages) may be produced.

9. Why does the percentage of students receiving additional resources for disadvantages differ from country to country?

This is the same question discussed above in Section 1 in the context of disabilities. Given that issues concerning those countries with no cross-national category C students have been discussed above in Section 7, this discussion focuses on differences in percentages between countries with such students.

- *Some countries provide additional resources for disadvantages which are not so resourced in other countries.* Inspection of Table 2.2 in Chapter 2 again illustrates the problems involved in assessing this possibility. The number, labelling, and definition of categories of disadvantages vary widely from country to country in a manner which obscures any linkage with overall proportions of students given additional resources.

- *Differences reflect policy differences.* Some countries may make the additional resourcing of students with disadvantages an educational priority. For instance, for a variety of reasons some countries may have more students living in poverty than others.

- *Numbers of migrants and others requiring additional resources because of linguistic problems differ from country to country.* Second language learning is an important component of the additional resources provided in countries with significant immigration but not for other countries.

10. Why does one country educate all students receiving additional resources for disadvantages in special schools, while all other countries for which data are available educate virtually all of them in regular classes with other students?

Five of the seven countries providing data for the period of compulsory education educate students with disadvantages almost exclusively in fully integrated settings. The picture is identical at all phases of education although data are patchy. The Slovak Republic provides the exception, educating all such students in special schools.

- *Differences reflect policy differences.* It appears highly likely that integration or segregation is a matter of national policy.

Policy action implications

The education of students from socially disadvantaged backgrounds is clearly a priority in most OECD countries. Increased levels of immigration underline this point. As for A and B, reviews of whether resources are adequate and whether they are being used appropriately for C students are called for. Consideration should be given to school organisation, teaching methods, teacher preparation and identification and outcomes for A, B and C students.

In general terms the effective education of students in A, B and C is predicated on changes in the way the education system functions for them and how education works with other services (*e.g.* OECD, 1995b, 1996, 1998a). Greater attention should be given at a holistic level to the issues identified above.

Gender

11. Why are more males than females receiving additional resources to help them access the curriculum?

The findings reported in the previous monographs (OECD, 2000b, 2004) concerning gender are fully replicated here. Breakdowns of gender by country, by location and level of education (pre-primary, primary, lower secondary and upper secondary) reveal that except in a few cases more boys than girls are receiving additional resources to access the curriculum. For those with disabilities the median percentage of males is 61.3% and for those with difficulties the median is 66.78%, while for disadvantages the range is typically between 50% and 60%. There is a statistically significant difference between the scores for students with disabilities and those with difficulties.

- *Males are more vulnerable than females.* There is some evidence that males are more vulnerable than females throughout the developmental years to the effects of illness and trauma. Thus they have a greater "natural" need for additional supports in school. This outcome would be seen as equitable since males objectively need more support.

- *The successful education of males is given greater social priority than that of females.* If this is the case then the failure or low performance of males in school is less acceptable than for females and extra resources are made available to lessen the effects and maximise performance. This outcome would be inequitable for females.

- *Males externalize their "feelings" in school more openly than females.* And in so-doing make themselves more likely to be identified and consequently labeled. Recent examples of extreme violence perpetrated by males in schools highlights the point.

- *Schooling is becoming increasingly "feminised".* The greater proportion of female teachers in schools especially during the primary years has been observed (OECD, 2002). Also the increased emphasis on the need for academic learning and the decreased need for standard "working class" skills may be moving schooling away from traditional types of male activity. The significant difference between males with disabilities and those with difficulties noted above may well mirror these issues.

Policy action implications

The fact that in most countries there are substantially more males than females receiving additional resources to help them access the curriculum needs reviewing on three counts.

- First, to establish what aspects of students' identification may bias decisions in favour of males.

- Second, what features of school functioning and decision-making may exacerbate problems thus bringing them to the attention of the "authorities".

- Third, whether the distribution of resources is equitable. That is, should more support be given to females?

Implications of the results of the third data collection exercise for future developments

The Electronic Questionnaire

The use of the Electronic Questionnaire (EQ) has been regarded as a considerable improvement by all concerned. By combining this with pre-entry of existing basic data from the previous exercise, completion of the task by data providers has been considerably simplified. It has also substantially reduced the size of the initial data entry task from an analysis perspective. The existence of mistakes, anomalies, miscodings, double entries, etc., continues with electronic entry, and the task of checking and general cleaning of the data set is formidable calling for substantial interaction with data providers. Such problems are inevitable given the complexity of the data entry task and its interpretation in the context of widely differing educational systems. However, increasing familiarity with the EQ in successive data collection exercises, together with further clarification of instructions and, where possible simplification of the data entry task, will be expected to reduce these problems.

Extension including pre-primary and all years of schooling

The extension of the scope of the exercise, beyond the central years of schooling, to pre-primary and upper secondary phases of education, can also be regarded as successful in the sense that it has garnered useful data. The extent of data availability at these levels is, as anticipated, not as great as at primary and lower secondary, but not markedly so. In passing, it is worth pointing out the value of requesting data on the period of compulsory education as a separate category (not a common feature of UOE data collection) as this typically leads to more countries being able to respond with data than for any other phase of education.

Limitations of current methodology

However, while pointing out the utility of extending from pre-primary to the full school range, it should be clearly acknowledged that the majority of countries taking part in this exercise have been unable to provide much of the data requested. The general conclusions of the first data collection exercise in this respect still stand – data availability for students with disabilities in segregated settings (particularly in special schools) is high; data availability for students receiving additional resources in integrated settings is very low. There have been improvements from the first exercise, particularly in relation to the availability of data on cross-national categories B and C (difficulties and disadvantages respectively). And through successive iterations previous anomalies in the allocation of national categories to B and C have been largely removed. However, it appears clear that the current methodology of asking for a central national response on students receiving additional resources in integrated settings (particularly in decentralised national systems) will not work. As discussed in Chapter 4, two countries have data (Canada [NB] and Italy) but for the most part data are either missing or the categories are declared not applicable for all phases of education.

Need for use of EQ at school and/or other sub-national levels

It appears very clear that an alternative methodology is called for. The obvious solution is what has been termed the "School Level Questionnaire"; *i.e.* a version of the EQ where data are collected at school level. This is attractive as it should not be difficult at the level of the individual school to provide data on students receiving additional resources, but it does present other problems (*e.g.* sampling issues; ensuring that local data providers understand the task). It may be that for different countries the optimum solution to the data gathering task is by an exercise based not on individual schools, but on a local administrative area, or a wider region of the country. Trials of this approach have been encouraging and it appears a matter of priority for proposals to be formulated and agreed to, in order to implement this more generally.

Extending collection of data on student gender

The earlier finding of an over-representation of males amongst students receiving additional resources is fully replicated. There are indications of systematic differences in the degree of over-representation, which give considerable promise in the attempt to interpret what lies behind this apparently inequitable distribution of resources.

However, the data coverage is currently insufficient to make trustworthy comparisons. Given the importance of this issue, and the relatively minor changes needed to collect data for males and females separately where total student numbers are currently collected, a clear priority exists for countries to make serious attempts to implement this in the next data collection exercise.

Modifications to the EQ

Need for continuity. It is taken as axiomatic that modifications to the type and form of data collected in the various data collection tables should be minimal. This is in part to avoid complicating and changing the task of data providers with their hard-won experience of completing the present EQ. It is also highly desirable that successive uses of the EQ help to build up comparable longitudinal data so that trends and changes can be examined.

Possible removal of areas with poor data yields. This does not preclude removal of parts of the EQ, particularly where it is clear that the approach of obtaining a central national response leads to poor data yields, as discussed above. However it would appear to be a step backwards to do this without setting in train the use of a different methodology (such as the School Level EQ) to provide an alternative route to collecting the required data.

Further efforts to obtain data on resources. A further problematic area with low yields is data on teachers. This is a valuable partial proxy for resources and it appears sensible to continue efforts to obtain these data. This may be another area where a separate exercise is called for, with the aim of extending the call for data to cover other professional and support staff as well as teachers (possibly as part of a wider initiative on the specification of resources).

Inclusion of post-school phase. Possible additions to the EQ include extending the range to include post-school tertiary education. Arguments for and against this are finely balanced. This aspect of education for students with disabilities, difficulties, and disadvantages is of considerable importance. However experience suggests the likely difficulty of getting worthwhile amounts of data using the EQ and it may be that a different, separate exercise is again called for.

Age distribution data. A further possible addition might be to call for separate data on cross-national categories A, B, and C in Table 6 on age distributions. Suggestions that misleading pictures were being presented when data on the three cross-national categories are combined (discussed in Chapter 4) led to their separate presentation in this monograph and it would be consistent to also do this for age distributions.

Final comments

The data gathered so far have been determined by what countries have available. Clearly this is an important starting point essential for the development of international comparisons. However, economic data and data on outcomes for students with disabilities, difficulties and disadvantages are at present in short supply, and future data collections will attempt to address these gaps if necessary through specific studies focusing on these two areas.

From the perspective of academic outcomes, the PISA study holds many possibilities. However, for these students other outcome variables are important. These include access to the labour market, entry into further or higher education, and domestic arrangements, either living at home or in care or elsewhere.

References

Department of Education (1997), *The Statistical Report of the Department of Education*, Dublin, Ireland.

Department of Education (1999), *The Statistical Report of the Department of Education*, Dublin, Ireland.

OECD (1993), "Access, Participation and Equity", OECD, Paris.

OECD (1995a), *Integrating Students with Special Needs into Mainstream Schools*, OECD, Paris.

OECD (1995b), *Our Children at Risk,* OECD, Paris.

OECD (1996), *Successful Services for our Children and Families at Risk,* OECD, Paris.

OECD (1998a), *Coordinating Services for Children and Youth at Risk. A World View*, OECD, Paris.

OECD (1998b), *Education at a Glance – OECD Indicators,* Paris.

OECD (1999), *Inclusive Education at Work: Including Students with Disabilities into Mainstream Schools*, OECD, Paris.

OECD (2000a), *Education at a Glance – OECD Indicators*, OECD, Paris.

OECD (2000b), *Special Needs Education – Statistics and Indicators*, OECD, Paris.

OECD (2002), *Education at a Glance – OECD Indicators*, OECD, Paris.

OECD (2003a), *Education at a Glance – OECD Indicators*, OECD, Paris.

OECD (2003b), *Education Policy Analysis*, OECD, Paris.

OECD (2004), *Equity in Education – Students with Disabilities, Learning Difficulties and Disadvantages*, OECD, Paris.

UNESCO (1997), *International Standard Classification of Education, ISCED*, UNESCO, Paris.

Annex 1
Distribution of individual national categories into 22 general categories used to describe students with disabilities, difficulties and disadvantages[1]

Country	Visual impairment	Blindness	Hearing impairment	Deafness	Emotional, behavioural difficulties	Severe learning problems	Moderate learning problems	Light learning problems	Physical disabilities	Combinatorial disabilities	Specific learning difficulties	Speech and language problems	Hospital	Other health problems	Autism	Gifted and talented students	Remedial help	2nd language and mother tongue teaching	Travelling children	Disadvantaged students	Aboriginal and indigenous students	Young offenders
Belgium (Fl.)	6x	6x	7x	7x	3	2x	2x	1	4		8, 11		5	9			10	12x, 13, 16, 17	14	12x		15
Belgium (Fr.)	6x	6x	7x	7x	3	2x	2x	1	4		8		5					11x		11x, 10, 12		9
Canada (NB)	4x	4x	4x	4x	1	3x	3x	3x	4x	6	3x, 5	2						7				
Czech Rep.	3x	3x	2x	2x	8x	1x	1x		5	6	8x	4	7	9, 10	12					11		
Finland	5x	5x	4x	4x	7, 15	3	2	1	6		10, 11, 12, 14	9		8			13, 16, 18	17				
France	9	8	7	6		1, 2	3		4	13	15	11						14		16		
Germany	2x	2x	3x	3x	7	6x	6x		5	9	1	4	8	10, 11	12		13	15	14			
Greece	1x	1x	2x	2x	6x	4x	4x	6x	3	7, 5x	6x	6x				5x		8x		8x		
Hungary	3x	3x	4x	4x	7x		2		5		1, 7x	6		7x	7x					8		
Italy	1x	1x	2x	2x		3x, 4	3x		5, 6	7								8x		8x		
Japan	1x	1x	2x	2x	7	3x	3x	3x	4			6		5				8				
Korea	1x	1x	2x	2x	5x	3x	3x	9x	4			7	6	8	5x							
Mexico	2	1	4	5		3x	3x	3x	6	7	8				9			11x	13	11x, 10	12	
Netherlands	4x	4x	2	1	7x, 9	8		13x	5	11	7x, 13x	3	10	6				12x		12x		
Poland	5	4	7	6	11, 12	2, 3, 17x	1		9	14	18x, 19x	8, 16x, 19x					13	15, 16x, 17x, 18x, 19x		10x		10x
Slovak Rep.	2x	2x	1x	1x	9, 10x	6	5		3	11	8	4	12		7							10x
Spain	3x	3x	1x	1x	5	4x	4x	4x	2	6	11	9				7		12		10	8	
Sweden	1x	1x	1x, 3x	1x		2x	2x		1x, 3x					5						4		
Switzerland	16x	16x	14x	14x	13, 4	9x, 10x	9x, 10x		12, 6	11, 18	1, 2, 3	7, 15	8, 17	19				5				
Turkey	1x	1x	2x	2x	11	5, 9,	4		3		10	6	8			13	7	12x		12x		
United States	3x	3x	10x	10x	4	1x, 12x	1x, 12x	13	5	8, 9	7	2		6	11					14		

1. Matrix of 22 national categories covering disadvantaged students provided with additional resources to access the curriculum, by country. Since not all countries use all categories there are many empty cells. The number in each cell refers to the number of that category for that particular country as given in Table 2.2. The "x" indicates that the category includes children from one or more of the other 22 categories and therefore on its own makes it non-comparable with a category containing only those children.

Annex 2
Data availability tables

Cross-national category A

	Special schools					Special classes					Regular classes				
	Compulsory school education	Pre-primary school education	Primary or basic school education	Lower secondary school education	Upper secondary school education	Compulsory school education	Pre-primary school education	Primary or basic school education	Lower secondary school education	Upper secondary school education	Compulsory school education	Pre-primary school education	Primary or basic school education	Lower secondary school education	Upper secondary school education
Belgium (Fr.)	✓	✓	✓	✓	x	a	a	a	a	a	m	m	m	m	m
Belgium (Fl.)	✓	✓	✓	✓	✓	a	a	a	a	a	✓	✓	✓	✓	x
Canada (NB)	a	a	a	a	a	a	a	a	a	a	✓	a	✓	✓	✓
Czech Rep.	✓	✓	✓	✓	✓	✓	✓	✓	✓	✓	✓	✓	✓	✓	✓
Finland	✓	✓	✓	✓	m:	✓	✓	✓	✓	m:	✓	✓	✓	✓	m:
France	✓	x	x	x	x	✓	a	✓	a	a	✓	m	✓	✓	✓
Germany	✓	a	x	x	x	x	x	x	x	x	✓	n	✓	✓	✓
Greece	✓	✓	✓	✓	x	✓	✓	✓	✓	x	m	m	m	m	m
Hungary	✓	✓	✓	✓	n	✓	n	✓	✓	n	✓	✓	✓	✓	m
Italy	m:	✓	✓	✓	✓	m:	✓	✓	✓	✓	m	m	m:	m:	m
Japan	✓	✓	✓	✓	✓	✓	a	✓	✓	n	✓	a	✓	✓	a
Korea	✓	✓	✓	✓	✓	✓	✓	✓	✓	✓	✓	✓	✓	✓	✓
Mexico	✓	✓	✓	✓	a	✓	✓	✓	✓	m	✓	✓	✓	✓	n
Netherlands	✓	✓	✓	✓	✓	a	a	a	a	a	✓	a	✓	✓	m
Poland	✓	✓	✓	✓	✓	m	m	m	m	m	m:	m	m:	m:	m
Slovak Rep.	✓	✓	✓	✓	✓	✓	✓	✓	✓	✓	✓	✓	✓	✓	✓
Spain	✓	✓	✓	✓	n	x	x	x	x	n	✓	✓	✓	✓	✓
Sweden	✓	✓	✓	✓	✓	a	a	a	a	a	✓	a	✓	✓	m:
Switzerland	✓	a	x	x	a	✓	a	x	x	a	m	a	m	m	a
Turkey	✓	✓	✓	a	✓	✓	a	✓	a	a	✓	✓	✓	a	✓
United Kingdom (Eng.)	✓	✓	✓	✓	✓	x	x	x	x	x	✓	✓	✓	✓	✓
United States	✓	✓	✓	✓	✓	✓	✓	✓	✓	✓	✓	✓	✓	✓	✓

Cross-national category B

	Special schools					Special classes					Regular classes				
	Compulsory school education	Pre-primary school education	Primary or basic school education	Lower secondary school education	Upper secondary school education	Compulsory school education	Pre-primary school education	Primary or basic school education	Lower secondary school education	Upper secondary school education	Compulsory school education	Pre-primary school education	Primary or basic school education	Lower secondary school education	Upper secondary school education
Belgium (Fr.)	✓	✓	✓	✓	x	a	a	a	a	a	a	a	a	a	a
Belgium (Fl.)	✓	✓	✓	✓	✓	a	a	a	a	a	✓	✓	m:	✓	x
Canada (NB)	a	a	a	a	a	a	a	a	a	a	✓	a	✓	✓	✓
Czech Rep.	✓	✓	✓	✓	a	✓	✓	✓	✓	a	✓	✓	✓	✓	✓
Finland	✓	n	✓	✓	✓	✓	✓	✓	✓	✓	✓	m:	✓	✓	✓
France	✓	a	✓	✓	✓	✓	a	✓	✓	m	a	a	a	a	a
Germany	✓	✓	x	x	x	x	x	x	x	x	✓	n	✓	✓	n
Greece	✓	n	✓	n	x	n	n	n	n	x	m	m	m	m	m
Hungary	✓	✓	✓	✓	n	✓	n	✓	✓	n	m	m	m	m	m
Italy	a	a	a	a	a	a	a	a	a	a	a	a	a	a	a
Japan	a	a	a	a	a	a	a	a	a	a	a	a	a	a	a
Korea	✓	✓	✓	✓	✓	✓	✓	✓	✓	✓	✓	✓	✓	✓	✓
Mexico	✓	✓	✓	✓	a	✓	✓	✓	✓	m	✓	✓	✓	✓	n
Netherlands	✓	✓	✓	m:	m:	✓	a	a	✓	a	✓	m	m	✓	m
Poland	m:	m:	m:	m:	m:	m:	m:	m:	m:	m	m:	m	m:	m:	m:
Slovak Rep.	n	n	n	n	n	✓	✓	✓	✓	n	✓	✓	✓	✓	✓
Spain	a	a	a	a	a	a	a	a	a	a	✓	✓	✓	✓	✓
Sweden	a	a	a	a	a	a	a	a	a	a	a	a	a	a	a
Switzerland	✓	a	x	x	a	✓	a	x	x	a	m	a	m	m	a
Turkey	✓	a	✓	a	a	a	a	a	a	a	✓	✓	✓	a	✓
United Kingdom (Eng.)	✓	✓	✓	✓	✓	x	x	x	x	x	✓	✓	✓	✓	✓
United States	✓	✓	✓	✓	✓	✓	✓	✓	✓	✓	✓	✓	✓	✓	✓

Cross-national category C															
	Special schools					Special classes					Regular classes				
	Compulsory school education	Pre-primary school education	Primary or basic school education	Lower secondary school education	Upper secondary school education	Compulsory school education	Pre-primary school education	Primary or basic school education	Lower secondary school education	Upper secondary school education	Compulsory school education	Pre-primary school education	Primary or basic school education	Lower secondary school education	Upper secondary school education
Belgium (Fr.)	a	a	a	a	a	m	m	m	m	m	m	x	m	x	✓
Belgium (Fl.)	a	a	a	a	a	✓	a	✓	✓	a	m:	m:	m:	m:	m:
Canada (NB)	a	a	a	a	a	a	a	a	a	a	✓	a	✓	✓	✓
Czech Rep.	✓	✓	✓	✓	✓	a	✓	a	a	a	m	m	m	m	m
Finland	a	a	a	a	a	a	a	a	a	a	✓	a	✓	✓	a
France	a	a	a	a	a	✓	n	✓	✓	✓	✓	✓	✓	✓	✓
Germany	a	a	a	a	a	x	x	x	x	x	a	a	a	a	a
Greece	✓	✓	✓	n	x	n	n	n	n	x	m	m	m	m	m
Hungary	a	a	a	a	a	a	a	a	a	a	a	a	a	a	a
Italy	a	a	a	a	a	n	n	n	n	n	m	✓	✓	✓	✓
Japan	m	n	✓	n	n	m	m	m	m	m	m	a	m	m	m
Korea	a	a	a	a	a	a	a	a	a	a	a	a	a	a	a
Mexico	✓	✓	✓	m	a	m	m	m	m	m	m:	m	m:	m:	a
Netherlands	a	a	a	a	a	a	a	a	a	a	✓	✓	✓	✓	✓
Poland	✓	n	✓	✓	✓	m	m	m	m	m	✓	m	✓	✓	m
Slovak Rep.	✓	✓	✓	✓	✓	n	n	n	n	n	n	n	n	n	n
Spain	n	n	n	n	n	a	a	a	a	a	✓	✓	✓	✓	n
Sweden	a	a	a	a	a	m	a	m	m	m	m:	m:	m:	m:	m
Switzerland	a	a	a	a	a	✓	a	x	x	a	m	m	m	m	a
Turkey	✓	a	✓	a	a	a	a	a	a	a	✓	✓	✓	a	✓
United Kingdom (Eng.)	a	a	a	a	a	a	a	a	a	a	a	a	a	a	a
United States	a	a	a	a	a	a	a	a	a	a	✓	m	✓	✓	m

Annex 3
Compulsory school education

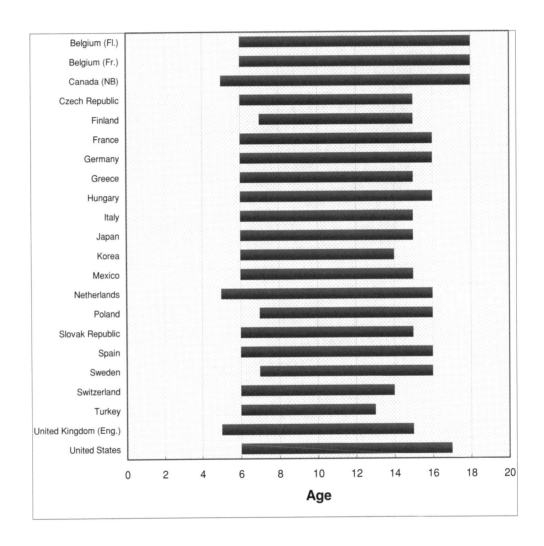

Also available in the CERI collection

E-learning in Tertiary Education: Where do We Stand?
290 pages • June 2005 • ISBN: 92-64-00920-5

Formative Assessment – Improving Learning in Secondary Classrooms
280 pages • February 2005 • ISBN: 92-64-00739-3

Internationalisation and Trade in Higher Education – *Opportunities and Challenges*
250 pages • June 2004 • ISBN: 92-64-01504-3

Innovation in the Knowledge Economy – *Implications for Education and Learning*
Knowledge Management series
96 pages • May 2004 • ISBN: 92-64-10560-3

Equity in Education – *Students with Disabilities, Learning Difficulties and Disadvantages*
165 pages • May 2004 • ISBN: 92-64-10368-6

Disability in Higher Education
168 pages • December 2003 • ISBN: 92-64-10505-0

Measuring Knowledge Management in the Business Sector: First Steps
Knowledge Management series
219 pages • December 2003 • ISBN: 92-64-10026-1

New Challenges for Educational Research
Knowledge Management series
146 pages • August 2003 • ISBN: 92-64-10030-X

Networks of Innovation – *Towards New Models for Managing Schools and Systems*
Schooling for Tomorrow series
182 pages • June 2003 • ISBN: 92-64-10034-2

Understanding the Brain – *Towards a New Learning Science*
115 pages • July 2002 • ISBN: 92-64-19734-6

www.oecdbookshop.org

OECD PUBLICATIONS, 2, rue André-Pascal, 75775 PARIS CEDEX 16
PRINTED IN FRANCE
(96 2005 05 1 P) ISBN 92-64-00980-9 – No. 53993 2005